PERSONA

M000228480

Name:
....

Address:
....

....

Telephone: Email:
....

Employer:
....

Address:
....

....

Telephone: Email:
....

MEDICAL INFORMATION

Physician: Telephone:
....

Allergies:
....

Medications:
....

Blood Type:
....

Insurer:
....

IN CASE OF EMERGENCY, NOTIFY

Name:
....

Address:
....

Telephone: Relationship:
....

Published by Barbour Publishing, Inc., 1810 Barbour Drive, Uhrichsville, Ohio 44683, www.barbourbooks.com

Our mission is to inspire the world with the life-changing message of the Bible.

Member of the
Evangelical Christian
Publishers Association

Printed in China.

God Made You for More

2023 Creative Planner

BARBOUR

PUBLISHING

Made for More

Whether you're battling through a season of bitterness, heart-ache, disappointment, fear, insecurity, regret, shame, or un-forgiveness, this creative planner—with creative, bulleted monthly journaling pages—will remind you that the heavenly Creator made you for *so much more*. As you plan each week of the year, you'll encounter inspiring truths and scripture selections that promise to renew and refresh your spirit with this timeless biblical truth: life in Christ is meant to be an exciting adventure!

This is your year. . .now go and live out His amazing plan for your life!

2023

JANUARY

S	M	T	W	T	F	S
1	2	3	4	5	6	7
8	9	10	11	12	13	14
15	16	17	18	19	20	21
22	23	24	25	26	27	28
29	30	31				

FEBRUARY

S	M	T	W	T	F	S
			1	2	3	4
5	6	7	8	9	10	11
12	13	14	15	16	17	18
19	20	21	22	23	24	25
26	27	28				

MAY

S	M	T	W	T	F	S
	1	2	3	4	5	6
7	8	9	10	11	12	13
14	15	16	17	18	19	20
21	22	23	24	25	26	27
28	29	30	31			

JUNE

S	M	T	W	T	F	S
				1	2	3
4	5	6	7	8	9	10
11	12	13	14	15	16	17
18	19	20	21	22	23	24
25	26	27	28	29	30	

SEPTEMBER

S	M	T	W	T	F	S
					1	2
3	4	5	6	7	8	9
10	11	12	13	14	15	16
17	18	19	20	21	22	23
24	25	26	27	28	29	30

OCTOBER

S	M	T	W	T	F	S
1	2	3	4	5	6	7
8	9	10	11	12	13	14
15	16	17	18	19	20	21
22	23	24	25	26	27	28
29	30	31				

Year *at a* Glance

MARCH

S	M	T	W	T	F	S
			1	2	3	4
5	6	7	8	9	10	11
12	13	14	15	16	17	18
19	20	21	22	23	24	25
26	27	28	29	30	31	

APRIL

S	M	T	W	T	F	S
						1
2	3	4	5	6	7	8
9	10	11	12	13	14	15
16	17	18	19	20	21	22
23	24	25	26	27	28	29
30						

JULY

S	M	T	W	T	F	S
						1
2	3	4	5	6	7	8
9	10	11	12	13	14	15
16	17	18	19	20	21	22
23	24	25	26	27	28	29
30	31					

AUGUST

S	M	T	W	T	F	S
		1	2	3	4	5
6	7	8	9	10	11	12
13	14	15	16	17	18	19
20	21	22	23	24	25	26
27	28	29	30	31		

NOVEMBER

S	M	T	W	T	F	S
			1	2	3	4
5	6	7	8	9	10	11
12	13	14	15	16	17	18
19	20	21	22	23	24	25
26	27	28	29	30		

DECEMBER

S	M	T	W	T	F	S
					1	2
3	4	5	6	7	8	9
10	11	12	13	14	15	16
17	18	19	20	21	22	23
24	25	26	27	28	29	30
31						

August 2022

SUNDAY	MONDAY	TUESDAY	WEDNESDAY
31	1	2	3
7	8	9	10
14	15	16	17
21	22	23	24
28	29	30	31

notes

THURSDAY	FRIDAY	SATURDAY
4	5	6
11	12	13
18	19	20
25	26	27
1	2	3

....
....
....
....
....
....
....
....
....
....
....
....
....

JULY

S	M	T	W	T	F	S
					1	2
3	4	5	6	7	8	9
10	11	12	13	14	15	16
17	18	19	20	21	22	23
24	25	26	27	28	29	30
31						

SEPTEMBER

S	M	T	W	T	F	S
				1	2	3
4	5	6	7	8	9	10
11	12	13	14	15	16	17
18	19	20	21	22	23	24
25	26	27	28	29	30	

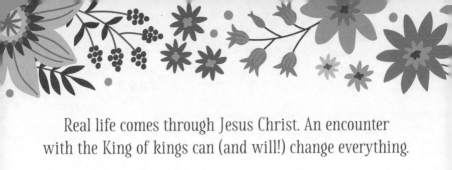

Real life comes through Jesus Christ. An encounter
with the King of kings can (and will!) change everything.

Goals *for* This Month

Jesus said to him, "I am the way, and the truth, and the life. No one comes to the Father except through me."

JOHN 14:6 ESV

July–August 2022

S	M	T	W	T	F	S
	1	2	3	4	5	6
7	8	9	10	11	12	13
14	15	16	17	18	19	20
21	22	23	24	25	26	27
28	29	30	31			

You were made to spend more time with your Creator; He longs for it and wants you to desire the same.

to-do list

- [ ] ....
- [ ] ....
- [ ] ....
- [ ] ....
- [ ] ....
- [ ] ....
- [ ] ....
- [ ] ....
- [ ] ....
- [ ] ....
- [ ] ....
- [ ] ....
- [ ] ....
- [ ] ....
- [ ] ....
- [ ] ....
- [ ] ....
- [ ] ....
- [ ] ....

SUNDAY, July 31

....
....
....
....
....

MONDAY, August 1

....
....
....
....
....

TUESDAY, August 2

....
....
....
....
....

WEDNESDAY, August 3

....
....
....
....
....

THURSDAY, August 4

....
....
....
....
....

FRIDAY, August 5

....
....
....
....
....

SATURDAY, August 6

....
....
....
....
....

to-do list

- [ ] ....
- [ ] ....
- [ ] ....
- [ ] ....
- [ ] ....
- [ ] ....
- [ ] ....
- [ ] ....
- [ ] ....
- [ ] ....
- [ ] ....
- [ ] ....
- [ ] ....
- [ ] ....
- [ ] ....
- [ ] ....

Draw near to God, and he will draw near to you.
JAMES 4:8 ESV

August 2022

S	M	T	W	T	F	S
	1	2	3	4	5	6
7	8	9	10	11	12	13
14	15	16	17	18	19	20
21	22	23	24	25	26	27
28	29	30	31			

You were made for so much more than your past. It's over—done with. God has forgiven you and set you free. Hallelujah!

to-do list

- [ ]
- [ ]
- [ ]
- [ ]
- [ ]
- [ ]
- [ ]
- [ ]
- [ ]
- [ ]
- [ ]
- [ ]
- [ ]
- [ ]
- [ ]
- [ ]
- [ ]
- [ ]

SUNDAY, August 7

MONDAY, August 8

TUESDAY, August 9

WEDNESDAY, August 10

....
....
....
....
....

THURSDAY, August 11

....
....
....
....
....

FRIDAY, August 12

....
....
....
....
....

SATURDAY, August 13

....
....
....
....
....

to-do list

☐ ....
☐ ....
☐ ....
☐ ....
☐ ....
☐ ....
☐ ....
☐ ....
☐ ....
☐ ....
☐ ....
☐ ....
☐ ....
☐ ....
☐ ....
☐ ....

*Listen to me,
O royal daughter;
take to heart what I say.*
PSALM 45:10 NLT

August 2022

S	M	T	W	T	F	S
	1	2	3	4	5	6
7	8	9	10	11	12	13
14	15	16	17	18	19	20
21	22	23	24	25	26	27
28	29	30	31			

Disappointments come no matter how much you wish them away. But you can take those disappointments to your heavenly Father and ask for His perspective. Ultimately, He has a terrific plan for you, and you can trust Him with the details.

to-do list

- ☐
- ☐
- ☐
- ☐
- ☐
- ☐
- ☐
- ☐
- ☐
- ☐
- ☐
- ☐
- ☐
- ☐
- ☐
- ☐
- ☐
- ☐
- ☐
- ☐

SUNDAY, August 14

MONDAY, August 15

TUESDAY, August 16

WEDNESDAY, August 17

....
....
....
....
....

THURSDAY, August 18

....
....
....
....
....

FRIDAY, August 19

....
....
....
....
....

SATURDAY, August 20

....
....
....
....
....

to-do list

- [ ] ....
- [ ] ....
- [ ] ....
- [ ] ....
- [ ] ....
- [ ] ....
- [ ] ....
- [ ] ....
- [ ] ....
- [ ] ....
- [ ] ....
- [ ] ....
- [ ] ....
- [ ] ....
- [ ] ....
- [ ] ....
- [ ] ....

Do not be anxious about anything, but in everything by prayer and supplication with thanksgiving let your requests be made known to God.
PHILIPPIANS 4:6 ESV

August 2022

S	M	T	W	T	F	S
	1	2	3	4	5	6
7	8	9	10	11	12	13
14	15	16	17	18	19	20
21	22	23	24	25	26	27
28	29	30	31			

You have nothing to fear; you were created for better things.

to-do list

- [ ] ....
- [ ] ....
- [ ] ....
- [ ] ....
- [ ] ....
- [ ] ....
- [ ] ....
- [ ] ....
- [ ] ....
- [ ] ....
- [ ] ....
- [ ] ....
- [ ] ....
- [ ] ....
- [ ] ....
- [ ] ....
- [ ] ....
- [ ] ....

SUNDAY, August 21

....
....
....
....
....

MONDAY, August 22

....
....
....
....
....

TUESDAY, August 23

....
....
....
....
....

WEDNESDAY, August 24

THURSDAY, August 25

FRIDAY, August 26

SATURDAY, August 27

to-do list

- [ ]
- [ ]
- [ ]
- [ ]
- [ ]
- [ ]
- [ ]
- [ ]
- [ ]
- [ ]
- [ ]
- [ ]
- [ ]
- [ ]
- [ ]
- [ ]
- [ ]

*I sought the LORD,
and he answered me
and delivered me
from all my fears.*
PSALM 34:4 ESV

August–September 2022

S	M	T	W	T	F	S
		1	2	3	4	5	6
7	8	9	10	11	12	13
14	15	16	17	18	19	20
21	22	23	24	25	26	27
28	29	30	31			

God calls you beautiful. He sees
no flaws when He looks at you!

to-do list

- ☐ ....
- ☐ ....
- ☐ ....
- ☐ ....
- ☐ ....
- ☐ ....
- ☐ ....
- ☐ ....
- ☐ ....
- ☐ ....
- ☐ ....
- ☐ ....
- ☐ ....
- ☐ ....
- ☐ ....
- ☐ ....
- ☐ ....

SUNDAY, August 28

....
....
....
....
....

MONDAY, August 29

....
....
....
....
....

TUESDAY, August 30

....
....
....
....
....

WEDNESDAY, August 31

to-do list

- [ ]
- [ ]
- [ ]
- [ ]
- [ ]

THURSDAY, September 1

- [ ]
- [ ]
- [ ]
- [ ]
- [ ]
- [ ]
- [ ]

FRIDAY, September 2

- [ ]
- [ ]
- [ ]
- [ ]
- [ ]

SATURDAY, September 3

*"Fear not, therefore;
you are of more value
than many sparrows."*
MATTHEW 10:31 ESV

September 2022

SUNDAY	MONDAY	TUESDAY	WEDNESDAY
28	29	30	31
4	5 *Labor Day*	6	7
11	12	13	14
18	19	20	21
25	26	27	28

THURSDAY	FRIDAY	SATURDAY
1	2	3
8	9	10
15	16	17
22 *First Day of Autumn*	23	24
29	30	1

notes

....
....
....
....
....
....
....
....
....
....
....
....

AUGUST

S	M	T	W	T	F	S
	1	2	3	4	5	6
7	8	9	10	11	12	13
14	15	16	17	18	19	20
21	22	23	24	25	26	27
28	29	30	31			

OCTOBER

S	M	T	W	T	F	S
						1
2	3	4	5	6	7	8
9	10	11	12	13	14	15
16	17	18	19	20	21	22
23	24	25	26	27	28	29
30	31					

God can take a situation–even an
extremely difficult one–and mend it.

Goals *for* This Month

*If we confess our sins, he is faithful and just to forgive
us our sins and to cleanse us from all unrighteousness.*

1 JOHN 1:9 ESV

September 2022

S	M	T	W	T	F	S
				1	2	3
4	5	6	7	8	9	10
11	12	13	14	15	16	17
18	19	20	21	22	23	24
25	26	27	28	29	30	

Forgive yourself. Whether your mistake was an accident or on purpose. No matter the consequences. No matter *who* or *what* or *where* or *when*. Allow God to wash you clean once and for all.

to-do list

☐ ....
☐ ....
☐ ....
☐ ....
☐ ....
☐ ....
☐ ....
☐ ....
☐ ....
☐ ....
☐ ....
☐ ....
☐ ....
☐ ....
☐ ....
☐ ....
☐ ....
☐ ....
☐ ....

SUNDAY, September 4

....
....
....
....
....

MONDAY, September 5   *Labor Day*

....
....
....
....
....

TUESDAY, September 6

....
....
....
....
....

WEDNESDAY, September 7

....
....
....
....
....

THURSDAY, September 8

....
....
....
....
....

FRIDAY, September 9

....
....
....
....
....

SATURDAY, September 10

....
....
....
....
....

to-do list

☐ ....
☐ ....
☐ ....
☐ ....
☐ ....
☐ ....
☐ ....
☐ ....
☐ ....
☐ ....
☐ ....
☐ ....
☐ ....
☐ ....

*Instead of your
shame there shall
be a double portion;
instead of dishonor
they shall rejoice in
their lot; therefore in
their land they shall
possess a double
portion; they shall
have everlasting joy.*
ISAIAH 61:7 ESV

September 2022

S	M	T	W	T	F	S
				1	2	3
4	5	6	7	8	9	10
11	12	13	14	15	16	17
18	19	20	21	22	23	24
25	26	27	28	29	30	

You were made for more than your suffering, sister—whether physical or emotional. No matter what label the world sticks on you, God calls you His precious daughter.

to-do list

- [ ]
- [ ]
- [ ]
- [ ]
- [ ]
- [ ]
- [ ]
- [ ]
- [ ]
- [ ]
- [ ]
- [ ]
- [ ]
- [ ]
- [ ]
- [ ]
- [ ]
- [ ]

SUNDAY, September 11

MONDAY, September 12

TUESDAY, September 13

WEDNESDAY, September 14

....

....

....

....

....

THURSDAY, September 15

....

....

....

....

....

FRIDAY, September 16

....

....

....

....

....

SATURDAY, September 17

....

....

....

....

....

to-do list

☐ ....
☐ ....
☐ ....
☐ ....
☐ ....
☐ ....
☐ ....
☐ ....
☐ ....
☐ ....
☐ ....
☐ ....
☐ ....

*We can rejoice, too,
when we run into
problems and trials, for
we know that they help
us develop endurance.
And endurance
develops strength
of character, and
character strengthens
our confident hope
of salvation.*

ROMANS 5:3-4 NLT

September 2022

S	M	T	W	T	F	S
				1	2	3
4	5	6	7	8	9	10
11	12	13	14	15	16	17
18	19	20	21	22	23	24
25	26	27	28	29	30	

Know and trust that God will *never* reject you. You're His precious child, and He created you to be included—by Him *and* His people.

to-do list

- [ ] ....
- [ ] ....
- [ ] ....
- [ ] ....
- [ ] ....
- [ ] ....
- [ ] ....
- [ ] ....
- [ ] ....
- [ ] ....
- [ ] ....
- [ ] ....
- [ ] ....
- [ ] ....
- [ ] ....
- [ ] ....
- [ ] ....
- [ ] ....

SUNDAY, September 18

....
....
....
....
....

MONDAY, September 19

....
....
....
....
....

TUESDAY, September 20

....
....
....
....
....

WEDNESDAY, September 21

....
....
....
....
....

THURSDAY, September 22   *First Day of Autumn*

....
....
....
....
....

FRIDAY, September 23

....
....
....
....
....

SATURDAY, September 24

....
....
....
....
....

to-do list

- [ ] ....
- [ ] ....
- [ ] ....
- [ ] ....
- [ ] ....
- [ ] ....
- [ ] ....
- [ ] ....
- [ ] ....
- [ ] ....
- [ ] ....
- [ ] ....
- [ ] ....
- [ ] ....
- [ ] ....
- [ ] ....
- [ ] ....
- [ ] ....

*No, God has not
rejected his own people,
whom he chose from
the very beginning.*
ROMANS 11:2 NLT

September–October 2022

S	M	T	W	T	F	S
				1	2	3
4	5	6	7	8	9	10
11	12	13	14	15	16	17
18	19	20	21	22	23	24
25	26	27	28	29	30	

Beautiful woman, God will *never* abandon you. You're His— forever. In His sight, you are chosen and precious *always*.

to-do list

- [ ] ....
- [ ] ....
- [ ] ....
- [ ] ....
- [ ] ....
- [ ] ....
- [ ] ....
- [ ] ....
- [ ] ....
- [ ] ....
- [ ] ....
- [ ] ....
- [ ] ....
- [ ] ....
- [ ] ....
- [ ] ....
- [ ] ....
- [ ] ....
- [ ] ....

SUNDAY, September 25

MONDAY, September 26

TUESDAY, September 27

WEDNESDAY, September 28

....
....
....
....
....

THURSDAY, September 29

....
....
....
....
....

FRIDAY, September 30

....
....
....
....
....

SATURDAY, October 1

....
....
....
....

to-do list

- [ ] ....
- [ ] ....
- [ ] ....
- [ ] ....
- [ ] ....
- [ ] ....
- [ ] ....
- [ ] ....
- [ ] ....
- [ ] ....
- [ ] ....
- [ ] ....
- [ ] ....
- [ ] ....
- [ ] ....
- [ ] ....

As you come to him, a living stone rejected by men but in the sight of God chosen and precious.
1 PETER 2:4 ESV

October 2022

SUNDAY	MONDAY	TUESDAY	WEDNESDAY
25	26	27	28
2	3	4	5
9	10	11	12
	Columbus Day		
16	17	18	19
23	24	25	26
30	*Halloween* 31		

THURSDAY	FRIDAY	SATURDAY
29	30	1
6	7	8
13	14	15
20	21	22
27	28	29

notes

....
....
....
....
....
....
....
....
....
....
....
....

SEPTEMBER

S	M	T	W	T	F	S
				1	2	3
4	5	6	7	8	9	10
11	12	13	14	15	16	17
18	19	20	21	22	23	24
25	26	27	28	29	30	

NOVEMBER

S	M	T	W	T	F	S
		1	2	3	4	5
6	7	8	9	10	11	12
13	14	15	16	17	18	19
20	21	22	23	24	25	26
27	28	29	30			

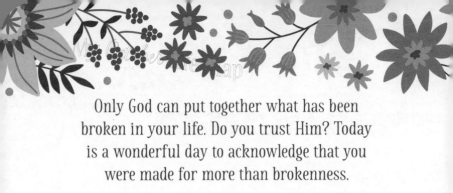

Only God can put together what has been broken in your life. Do you trust Him? Today is a wonderful day to acknowledge that you were made for more than brokenness.

Goals *for* This Month

"I have told you all this so that you may have peace in me. Here on earth you will have many trials and sorrows. But take heart, because I have overcome the world."

JOHN 16:33 NLT

October 2022

S	M	T	W	T	F	S
						1
2	3	4	5	6	7	8
9	10	11	12	13	14	15
16	17	18	19	20	21	22
23	24	25	26	27	28	29
30	31					

Respond to the heavenly Creator's daily miracles with the awe they deserve! Look out the window. Nature beckons you to respond in adoration to the Master Creator.

to-do list

☐ ....
☐ ....
☐ ....
☐ ....
☐ ....
☐ ....
☐ ....
☐ ....
☐ ....
☐ ....
☐ ....
☐ ....
☐ ....
☐ ....
☐ ....
☐ ....
☐ ....
☐ ....
☐ ....

SUNDAY, October 2

....
....
....
....
....

MONDAY, October 3

....
....
....
....
....

TUESDAY, October 4

....
....
....
....
....

WEDNESDAY, October 5

THURSDAY, October 6

FRIDAY, October 7

SATURDAY, October 8

to-do list

☐ ....
☐ ....
☐ ....
☐ ....
☐ ....
☐ ....
☐ ....
☐ ....
☐ ....
☐ ....
☐ ....
☐ ....
☐ ....

"But ask the beasts, and
they will teach you; the
birds of the heavens,
and they will tell you;
or the bushes of the
earth, and they will
teach you; and the fish
of the sea will declare
to you. Who among all
these does not know
that the hand of the
LORD has done this?"

JOB 12:7–9 ESV

October 2022

S	M	T	W	T	F	S
						1
2	3	4	5	6	7	8
9	10	11	12	13	14	15
16	17	18	19	20	21	22
23	24	25	26	27	28	29
30	31					

God designed you to be
authentically you. No one else.

to-do list

☐ ....
☐ ....
☐ ....
☐ ....
☐ ....
☐ ....
☐ ....
☐ ....
☐ ....
☐ ....
☐ ....
☐ ....
☐ ....
☐ ....
☐ ....
☐ ....
☐ ....

SUNDAY, October 9

....
....
....
....
....

MONDAY, October 10   *Columbus Day*

....
....
....
....
....

TUESDAY, October 11

....
....
....
....
....

WEDNESDAY, October 12

....
....
....
....
....

THURSDAY, October 13

....
....
....
....
....

FRIDAY, October 14

....
....
....
....
....

SATURDAY, October 15

....
....
....
....
....

to-do list

- [ ] ....
- [ ] ....
- [ ] ....
- [ ] ....
- [ ] ....
- [ ] ....
- [ ] ....
- [ ] ....
- [ ] ....
- [ ] ....
- [ ] ....
- [ ] ....
- [ ] ....
- [ ] ....
- [ ] ....

For our boast is this, the testimony of our conscience, that we behaved in the world with simplicity and godly sincerity, not by earthly wisdom but by the grace of God, and supremely so toward you.

2 CORINTHIANS 1:12 ESV

October 2022

S	M	T	W	T	F	S
						1
2	3	4	5	6	7	8
9	10	11	12	13	14	15
16	17	18	19	20	21	22
23	24	25	26	27	28	29
30	31					

The Lord created you for more—in every season, good and bad. No matter where you are right now, you can trust Him to provide everything you need and more.

to-do list

- [ ]
- [ ]
- [ ]
- [ ]
- [ ]
- [ ]
- [ ]
- [ ]
- [ ]
- [ ]
- [ ]
- [ ]
- [ ]
- [ ]
- [ ]
- [ ]
- [ ]
- [ ]

SUNDAY, October 16

MONDAY, October 17

TUESDAY, October 18

WEDNESDAY, October 19

....
....
....
....
....

THURSDAY, October 20

....
....
....
....
....

FRIDAY, October 21

....
....
....
....
....

SATURDAY, October 22

....
....
....
....
....

to-do list

- [ ] ....
- [ ] ....
- [ ] ....
- [ ] ....
- [ ] ....
- [ ] ....
- [ ] ....
- [ ] ....
- [ ] ....
- [ ] ....
- [ ] ....
- [ ] ....
- [ ] ....
- [ ] ....
- [ ] ....
- [ ] ....
- [ ] ....

*In this you rejoice,
though now for a little
while, if necessary, you
have been grieved
by various trials.*
1 PETER 1:6 ESV

October 2022

S	M	T	W	T	F	S
						1
2	3	4	5	6	7	8
9	10	11	12	13	14	15
16	17	18	19	20	21	22
23	24	25	26	27	28	29
30	31					

You are MORE. More faith. More hope. More joy. More kindness to others. More of a blessing to those in need. More dedicated to spreading the Word.

to-do list

☐ ....
☐ ....
☐ ....
☐ ....
☐ ....
☐ ....
☐ ....
☐ ....
☐ ....
☐ ....
☐ ....
☐ ....
☐ ....
☐ ....
☐ ....
☐ ....
☐ ....
☐ ....

SUNDAY, October 23

....
....
....
....
....

MONDAY, October 24

....
....
....
....

TUESDAY, October 25

....
....
....
....

WEDNESDAY, October 26

....
....
....
....
....

THURSDAY, October 27

....
....
....
....
....

FRIDAY, October 28

....
....
....
....
....

SATURDAY, October 29

....
....
....
....
....

to-do list

- [ ] ....
- [ ] ....
- [ ] ....
- [ ] ....
- [ ] ....
- [ ] ....
- [ ] ....
- [ ] ....
- [ ] ....
- [ ] ....
- [ ] ....
- [ ] ....
- [ ] ....
- [ ] ....
- [ ] ....
- [ ] ....
- [ ] ....

*"Now when these things
begin to take place,
straighten up and raise
your heads, because
your redemption is
drawing near."*

LUKE 21:28 ESV

November 2022

SUNDAY	MONDAY	TUESDAY	WEDNESDAY
30	31	1	2
6 *Daylight Saving Time Ends*	7	8 *Election Day*	9
13	14	15	16
20	21	22	23
27	28	28	30

notes

THURSDAY	FRIDAY	SATURDAY
3	4	5
10	11 *Veterans Day*	12
17	18	19
24 *Thanksgiving*	25	26
1	2	3

....
....
....
....
....
....
....
....
....
....
....
....

OCTOBER

S	M	T	W	T	F	S
						1
2	3	4	5	6	7	8
9	10	11	12	13	14	15
16	17	18	19	20	21	22
23	24	25	26	27	28	29
30	31					

DECEMBER

S	M	T	W	T	F	S
				1	2	3
4	5	6	7	8	9	10
11	12	13	14	15	16	17
18	19	20	21	22	23	24
25	26	27	28	29	30	31

That anticipation of "more than you could ask or think" is straight from heaven. God has promised it to you in His Word.

Goals *for* This Month

Now all glory to God, who is able, through his mighty power at work within us, to accomplish infinitely more than we might ask or think.

EPHESIANS 3:20 NLT

October–November 2022

S	M	T	W	T	F	S
			1	2	3	4	5
6	7	8	9	10	11	12
13	14	15	16	17	18	19
20	21	22	23	24	25	26
27	28	29	30			

God didn't intend for you to do life alone. The more you hang out with other believers, the stronger you'll become.

to-do list

- ☐ ....
- ☐ ....
- ☐ ....
- ☐ ....
- ☐ ....
- ☐ ....
- ☐ ....
- ☐ ....
- ☐ ....
- ☐ ....
- ☐ ....
- ☐ ....
- ☐ ....
- ☐ ....
- ☐ ....
- ☐ ....

SUNDAY, October 30

....
....
....
....
....

MONDAY, October 31   *Halloween*

....
....
....
....
....

TUESDAY, November 1

....
....
....
....
....

WEDNESDAY, November 2

....
....
....
....
....

THURSDAY, November 3

....
....
....
....
....

FRIDAY, November 4

....
....
....
....
....

SATURDAY, November 5

....
....
....
....
....

to-do list

- [ ] ....
- [ ] ....
- [ ] ....
- [ ] ....
- [ ] ....
- [ ] ....
- [ ] ....
- [ ] ....
- [ ] ....
- [ ] ....
- [ ] ....
- [ ] ....
- [ ] ....
- [ ] ....

*Let us consider how
to stir up one another
to love and good
works, not neglecting
to meet together, as
is the habit of some,
but encouraging one
another, and all the
more as you see the
Day drawing near.*
HEBREWS 10:24–25 ESV

November 2022

S	M	T	W	T	F	S
		1	2	3	4	5
6	7	8	9	10	11	12
13	14	15	16	17	18	19
20	21	22	23	24	25	26
27	28	29	30			

Where are you now? Is your "happily ever after" being crowded out by pain? Take a deep breath. Ask God to take your fears and channel them into something amazing, something long lasting.

to-do list

- ☐ ....
- ☐ ....
- ☐ ....
- ☐ ....
- ☐ ....
- ☐ ....
- ☐ ....
- ☐ ....
- ☐ ....
- ☐ ....
- ☐ ....
- ☐ ....
- ☐ ....
- ☐ ....
- ☐ ....
- ☐ ....
- ☐ ....
- ☐ ....

SUNDAY, November 6   *Daylight Saving Time Ends*

....
....
....
....
....

MONDAY, November 7

....
....
....
....
....

TUESDAY, November 8   *Election Day*

....
....
....
....
....

WEDNESDAY, November 9

to-do list

THURSDAY, November 10

FRIDAY, November 11   *Veterans Day*

SATURDAY, November 12

There is no fear in love. Perfect love puts fear out of our hearts. People have fear when they are afraid of being punished. The man who is afraid does not have perfect love.
1 JOHN 4:18 NLV

November 2022

S	M	T	W	T	F	S
		1	2	3	4	5
6	7	8	9	10	11	12
13	14	15	16	17	18	19
20	21	22	23	24	25	26
27	28	29	30			

No matter what you're walking through, God longs to reveal more of Himself to you today.

to-do list

☐ ....
☐ ....
☐ ....
☐ ....
☐ ....
☐ ....
☐ ....
☐ ....
☐ ....
☐ ....
☐ ....
☐ ....
☐ ....
☐ ....
☐ ....
☐ ....
☐ ....
☐ ....
☐ ....

SUNDAY, November 13

....
....
....
....
....

MONDAY, November 14

....
....
....
....
....

TUESDAY, November 15

....
....
....
....
....

WEDNESDAY, November 16

THURSDAY, November 17

FRIDAY, November 18

SATURDAY, November 19

to-do list

☐
☐
☐
☐
☐
☐
☐
☐
☐
☐
☐
☐
☐
☐
☐

I want to know Him. I want to have the same power in my life that raised Jesus from the dead. I want to understand and have a share in His sufferings and be like Christ in His death.
PHILIPPIANS 3:10 NLV

November 2022

S	M	T	W	T	F	S
		1	2	3	4	5
6	7	8	9	10	11	12
13	14	15	16	17	18	19
20	21	22	23	24	25	26
27	28	29	30			

The world is filled with broken
people yearning for wholeness.
Along the way, they need people
like you—people who are made for a
passionate response to the broken.

to-do list

☐ ....
☐ ....
☐ ....
☐ ....
☐ ....
☐ ....
☐ ....
☐ ....
☐ ....
☐ ....
☐ ....
☐ ....
☐ ....
☐ ....
☐ ....
☐ ....
☐ ....
☐ ....

SUNDAY, November 20

....
....
....
....
....

MONDAY, November 21

....
....
....
....
....

TUESDAY, November 22

....
....
....
....
....

WEDNESDAY, November 23

....
....
....
....
....

THURSDAY, November 24   *Thanksgiving Day*

....
....
....
....
....

FRIDAY, November 25

....
....
....
....
....

SATURDAY, November 26

....
....
....
....
....

to-do list

- [ ] ....
- [ ] ....
- [ ] ....
- [ ] ....
- [ ] ....
- [ ] ....
- [ ] ....
- [ ] ....
- [ ] ....
- [ ] ....
- [ ] ....
- [ ] ....
- [ ] ....
- [ ] ....
- [ ] ....
- [ ] ....

*The LORD is near to
the brokenhearted
and saves the
crushed in spirit.*
PSALM 34:18 ESV

November–December 2022

S	M	T	W	T	F	S
		1	2	3	4	5
6	7	8	9	10	11	12
13	14	15	16	17	18	19
20	21	22	23	24	25	26
27	28	29	30			

God created you to experience true joy—on good days and bad. Perhaps that's one reason laughter and tears are so closely connected.

to-do list

- [ ] ....
- [ ] ....
- [ ] ....
- [ ] ....
- [ ] ....
- [ ] ....
- [ ] ....
- [ ] ....
- [ ] ....
- [ ] ....
- [ ] ....
- [ ] ....
- [ ] ....
- [ ] ....
- [ ] ....
- [ ] ....
- [ ] ....
- [ ] ....

SUNDAY, November 27

MONDAY, November 28

TUESDAY, November 29

WEDNESDAY, November 30

....
....
....
....
....

THURSDAY, December 1

....
....
....
....
....

FRIDAY, December 2

....
....
....
....
....

SATURDAY, December 3

....
....
....
....
....

to-do list

- [ ] ....
- [ ] ....
- [ ] ....
- [ ] ....
- [ ] ....
- [ ] ....
- [ ] ....
- [ ] ....
- [ ] ....
- [ ] ....
- [ ] ....
- [ ] ....
- [ ] ....
- [ ] ....
- [ ] ....
- [ ] ....
- [ ] ....
- [ ] ....

"So also you have sorrow now, but I will see you again, and your hearts will rejoice, and no one will take your joy from you."
JOHN 16:22 ESV

December 2022

SUNDAY	MONDAY	TUESDAY	WEDNESDAY
27	28	29	30
4	5	6	7
11	12	13	14
18 *Hanukkah Begins at Sundown*	19	20	21 *First Day of Winter*
25 *Christmas Day*	26	27	28

notes

THURSDAY	FRIDAY	SATURDAY
1	2	3
8	9	10
15	16	17
22	23	24 *Christmas Eve*
29	30	31 *New Year's Eve*

NOVEMBER

S	M	T	W	T	F	S
		1	2	3	4	5
6	7	8	9	10	11	12
13	14	15	16	17	18	19
20	21	22	23	24	25	26
27	28	29	30			

JANUARY

S	M	T	W	T	F	S
1	2	3	4	5	6	7
8	9	10	11	12	13	14
15	16	17	18	19	20	21
22	23	24	25	26	27	28
29	30	31				

You were made to spend time in God's Word. God created you with a need, a desire, to know Him more, and part of the "knowing" comes by getting out your Bible and reading.

Goals *for* This Month

*So then faith cometh by hearing,
and hearing by the word of God.*
ROMANS 10:17 KJV

December 2022

S	M	T	W	T	F	S
				1	2	3
4	5	6	7	8	9	10
11	12	13	14	15	16	17
18	19	20	21	22	23	24
25	26	27	28	29	30	31

God gives strength to the powerless. Not just any kind of strength, mind you, but supernatural strength. One drop of the Creator's strength, and you're ready to tackle giants!

to-do list

- [ ] ....
- [ ] ....
- [ ] ....
- [ ] ....
- [ ] ....
- [ ] ....
- [ ] ....
- [ ] ....
- [ ] ....
- [ ] ....
- [ ] ....
- [ ] ....
- [ ] ....
- [ ] ....
- [ ] ....
- [ ] ....
- [ ] ....
- [ ] ....
- [ ] ....

SUNDAY, December 4

MONDAY, December 5

TUESDAY, December 6

WEDNESDAY, December 7

....

....

....

....

....

THURSDAY, December 8

....

....

....

....

....

FRIDAY, December 9

....

....

....

....

....

SATURDAY, December 10

....

....

....

....

....

to-do list

☐ ....
☐ ....
☐ ....
☐ ....
☐ ....
☐ ....
☐ ....
☐ ....
☐ ....
☐ ....
☐ ....
☐ ....
☐ ....
☐ ....
☐ ....
☐ ....
☐ ....

*He gives power to the
weak and strength
to the powerless.*
ISAIAH 40:29 NLT

December 2022

S	M	T	W	T	F	S
				1	2	3
4	5	6	7	8	9	10
11	12	13	14	15	16	17
18	19	20	21	22	23	24
25	26	27	28	29	30	31

You were made for more than work anxieties. God wants you to lay those down and rest in Him. No stress. No angst. Just complete and total relaxation.

to-do list

- [ ] ....
- [ ] ....
- [ ] ....
- [ ] ....
- [ ] ....
- [ ] ....
- [ ] ....
- [ ] ....
- [ ] ....
- [ ] ....
- [ ] ....
- [ ] ....
- [ ] ....
- [ ] ....
- [ ] ....
- [ ] ....
- [ ] ....
- [ ] ....

SUNDAY, December 11

....
....
....
....
....

MONDAY, December 12

....
....
....
....
....

TUESDAY, December 13

....
....
....
....
....

WEDNESDAY, December 14

....
....
....
....
....

THURSDAY, December 15

....
....
....
....
....

FRIDAY, December 16

....
....
....
....
....

SATURDAY, December 17

....
....
....
....
....

to-do list

☐ ....
☐ ....
☐ ....
☐ ....
☐ ....
☐ ....
☐ ....
☐ ....
☐ ....
☐ ....
☐ ....
☐ ....
☐ ....
☐ ....
☐ ....
☐ ....
☐ ....

*Cast all your anxiety
on him because he
cares for you.*
1 PETER 5:7 NIV

December 2022

S	M	T	W	T	F	S
				1	2	3
4	5	6	7	8	9	10
11	12	13	14	15	16	17
18	19	20	21	22	23	24
25	26	27	28	29	30	31

Are you a hearer or a doer? Only you can answer that question. But either way, you were created to be a doer.

to-do list

- [ ] ....
- [ ] ....
- [ ] ....
- [ ] ....
- [ ] ....
- [ ] ....
- [ ] ....
- [ ] ....
- [ ] ....
- [ ] ....
- [ ] ....
- [ ] ....
- [ ] ....
- [ ] ....
- [ ] ....
- [ ] ....
- [ ] ....
- [ ] ....

SUNDAY, December 18   *Hanukkah Begins at Sundown*

....
....
....
....
....

MONDAY, December 19

....
....
....
....
....

TUESDAY, December 20

....
....
....
....
....

WEDNESDAY, December 21 *First Day of Winter*

THURSDAY, December 22

FRIDAY, December 23

SATURDAY, December 24 *Christmas Eve*

to-do list

☐ ....
☐ ....
☐ ....
☐ ....
☐ ....
☐ ....
☐ ....
☐ ....
☐ ....
☐ ....
☐ ....
☐ ....
☐ ....
☐ ....
☐ ....
☐ ....

*Do not merely listen
to the word, and so
deceive yourselves.
Do what it says.*
JAMES 1:22 NIV

December 2022

S	M	T	W	T	F	S
				1	2	3
4	5	6	7	8	9	10
11	12	13	14	15	16	17
18	19	20	21	22	23	24
25	26	27	28	29	30	31

God commands us to love. In fact, He designed us to love. And He *expects* us to love, even when it feels impossible.

to-do list

- [ ] ....
- [ ] ....
- [ ] ....
- [ ] ....
- [ ] ....
- [ ] ....
- [ ] ....
- [ ] ....
- [ ] ....
- [ ] ....
- [ ] ....
- [ ] ....
- [ ] ....
- [ ] ....
- [ ] ....
- [ ] ....
- [ ] ....
- [ ] ....

SUNDAY, December 25   *Christmas Day*

....

....

....

....

....

MONDAY, December 26

....

....

....

....

....

TUESDAY, December 27

....

....

....

....

....

WEDNESDAY, December 28

....
....
....
....
....

THURSDAY, December 29

....
....
....
....
....

FRIDAY, December 30

....
....
....
....
....

SATURDAY, December 31   *New Year's Eve*

....
....
....
....
....

to-do list

☐ ....
☐ ....
☐ ....
☐ ....
☐ ....
☐ ....
☐ ....
☐ ....
☐ ....
☐ ....
☐ ....
☐ ....
☐ ....
☐ ....
☐ ....
☐ ....
☐ ....

*Above all, love each
other deeply, because
love covers over a
multitude of sins.*
1 PETER 4:8 NIV

January 2023

SUNDAY	MONDAY	TUESDAY	WEDNESDAY
1 *New Year's Day*	2	3	4
8	9	10	11
15	16 *Martin Luther King Jr. Day*	17	18
22	23	24	25
29	30	31	1

notes

THURSDAY	FRIDAY	SATURDAY
5	6	7
12	13	14
19	20	21
26	27	28
2	3	4

....
....
....
....
....
....
....
....
....
....
....
....
....

DECEMBER

S	M	T	W	T	F	S
				1	2	3
4	5	6	7	8	9	10
11	12	13	14	15	16	17
18	19	20	21	22	23	24
25	26	27	28	29	30	31

FEBRUARY

S	M	T	W	T	F	S
			1	2	3	4
5	6	7	8	9	10	11
12	13	14	15	16	17	18
19	20	21	22	23	24	25
26	27	28				

Prayer time is share time. You share your heart,
and God shares His. It's a mutual conversation
that will draw you closer together.

Goals *for* This Month

Rejoice always, pray continually, give thanks in all circumstances; for this is God's will for you in Christ Jesus.
1 Thessalonians 5:16-18 niv

January 2023

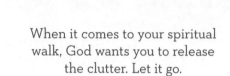

S	M	T	W	T	F	S
1	2	3	4	5	6	7
8	9	10	11	12	13	14
15	16	17	18	19	20	21
22	23	24	25	26	27	28
29	30	31				

When it comes to your spiritual walk, God wants you to release the clutter. Let it go.

to-do list

☐ ....
☐ ....
☐ ....
☐ ....
☐ ....
☐ ....
☐ ....
☐ ....
☐ ....
☐ ....
☐ ....
☐ ....
☐ ....
☐ ....
☐ ....
☐ ....
☐ ....
☐ ....

SUNDAY, January 1   *New Year's Day*

....
....
....
....
....

MONDAY, January 2

....
....
....
....
....

TUESDAY, January 3

....
....
....
....
....

WEDNESDAY, January 4

....
....
....
....
....

THURSDAY, January 5

....
....
....
....
....

FRIDAY, January 6

....
....
....
....
....

SATURDAY, January 7

....
....
....
....
....

to-do list

☐ ....
☐ ....
☐ ....
☐ ....
☐ ....
☐ ....
☐ ....
☐ ....
☐ ....
☐ ....
☐ ....
☐ ....
☐ ....
☐ ....
☐ ....
☐ ....

Therefore, if anyone is in Christ, the new creation has come: The old has gone, the new is here!
2 CORINTHIANS 5:17 NIV

January 2023

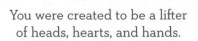

S	M	T	W	T	F	S
1	2	3	4	5	6	7
8	9	10	11	12	13	14
15	16	17	18	19	20	21
22	23	24	25	26	27	28
29	30	31				

You were created to be a lifter
of heads, hearts, and hands.

to-do list

☐ ....
☐ ....
☐ ....
☐ ....
☐ ....
☐ ....
☐ ....
☐ ....
☐ ....
☐ ....
☐ ....
☐ ....
☐ ....
☐ ....
☐ ....
☐ ....
☐ ....
☐ ....
☐ ....

SUNDAY, January 8

....
....
....
....
....

MONDAY, January 9

....
....
....
....
....

TUESDAY, January 10

....
....
....
....
....

WEDNESDAY, January 11

....
....
....
....
....

THURSDAY, January 12

....
....
....
....
....

FRIDAY, January 13

....
....
....
....
....

SATURDAY, January 14

....
....
....
....
....

to-do list

- [ ] ....
- [ ] ....
- [ ] ....
- [ ] ....
- [ ] ....
- [ ] ....
- [ ] ....
- [ ] ....
- [ ] ....
- [ ] ....
- [ ] ....
- [ ] ....
- [ ] ....
- [ ] ....
- [ ] ....
- [ ] ....

Two are better than one, because they have a good return for their labor: If either of them falls down, one can help the other up. But pity anyone who falls and has no one to help them up.
ECCLESIASTES 4:9-10 NIV

January 2023

S	M	T	W	T	F	S
1	2	3	4	5	6	7
8	9	10	11	12	13	14
15	16	17	18	19	20	21
22	23	24	25	26	27	28
29	30	31				

Don't give up. Keep hope alive, and look to the future as a brighter place. With the Lord's hand in yours, it surely will be.

to-do list

- [ ]
- [ ]
- [ ]
- [ ]
- [ ]
- [ ]
- [ ]
- [ ]
- [ ]
- [ ]
- [ ]
- [ ]
- [ ]
- [ ]
- [ ]
- [ ]
- [ ]
- [ ]
- [ ]

SUNDAY, January 15

MONDAY, January 16   *Martin Luther King Jr. Day*

TUESDAY, January 17

WEDNESDAY, January 18

....
....
....
....
....

THURSDAY, January 19

....
....
....
....
....

FRIDAY, January 20

....
....
....
....
....

SATURDAY, January 21

....
....
....
....
....

to-do list

- [ ] ....
- [ ] ....
- [ ] ....
- [ ] ....
- [ ] ....
- [ ] ....
- [ ] ....
- [ ] ....
- [ ] ....
- [ ] ....
- [ ] ....
- [ ] ....
- [ ] ....
- [ ] ....
- [ ] ....
- [ ] ....
- [ ] ....
- [ ] ....

"For I know the plans I have for you," says the LORD. "They are plans for good and not for disaster, to give you a future and a hope."
JEREMIAH 29:11 NLT

January 2023

S	M	T	W	T	F	S
1	2	3	4	5	6	7
8	9	10	11	12	13	14
15	16	17	18	19	20	21
22	23	24	25	26	27	28
29	30	31				

Your desire to comfort others comes straight from the heart of your heavenly Father. He placed it inside of you so that others could sense His love and compassion through you.

to-do list

- [ ] ....
- [ ] ....
- [ ] ....
- [ ] ....
- [ ] ....
- [ ] ....
- [ ] ....
- [ ] ....
- [ ] ....
- [ ] ....
- [ ] ....
- [ ] ....
- [ ] ....
- [ ] ....
- [ ] ....
- [ ] ....
- [ ] ....
- [ ] ....

SUNDAY, January 22

MONDAY, January 23

TUESDAY, January 24

WEDNESDAY, January 25

....
....
....
....
....

THURSDAY, January 26

....
....
....
....
....

FRIDAY, January 27

....
....
....
....
....

SATURDAY, January 28

....
....
....
....
....

to-do list

- [ ] ....
- [ ] ....
- [ ] ....
- [ ] ....
- [ ] ....
- [ ] ....
- [ ] ....
- [ ] ....
- [ ] ....
- [ ] ....
- [ ] ....
- [ ] ....
- [ ] ....
- [ ] ....
- [ ] ....
- [ ] ....

*"I will comfort you
there in Jerusalem
as a mother comforts
her child."*
ISAIAH 66:13 NLT

February 2023

SUNDAY	MONDAY	TUESDAY	WEDNESDAY
29	30	31	1
5	6	7	8
12	13	14 *Valentine's Day*	15
19	20 *Presidents Day*	21	22 *Ash Wednesday*
26	27	28	1

notes

THURSDAY	FRIDAY	SATURDAY
2	3	4
9	10	11
16	17	18
23	24	25
2	3	4

....
....
....
....
....
....
....
....
....
....
....
....
....

JANUARY

S	M	T	W	T	F	S
1	2	3	4	5	6	7
8	9	10	11	12	13	14
15	16	17	18	19	20	21
22	23	24	25	26	27	28
29	30	31				

MARCH

S	M	T	W	T	F	S
			1	2	3	4
5	6	7	8	9	10	11
12	13	14	15	16	17	18
19	20	21	22	23	24	25
26	27	28	29	30	31	

Where there is fear, God will give
courage. Faith will rise up.

Goals *for* This Month

You have armed me with strength for the battle;
you have subdued my enemies under my feet.
PSALM 18:39 NLT

January–February 2023

S	M	T	W	T	F	S
			1	2	3	4
5	6	7	8	9	10	11
12	13	14	15	16	17	18
19	20	21	22	23	24	25
26	27	28				

God created you to be more than a shadow dweller when mountains rise in your path. You can speak to those mountains and watch them disappear into the sea!

to-do list

- [ ] ....
- [ ] ....
- [ ] ....
- [ ] ....
- [ ] ....
- [ ] ....
- [ ] ....
- [ ] ....
- [ ] ....
- [ ] ....
- [ ] ....
- [ ] ....
- [ ] ....
- [ ] ....
- [ ] ....
- [ ] ....
- [ ] ....
- [ ] ....

SUNDAY, January 29

....
....
....
....
....

MONDAY, January 30

....
....
....
....
....

TUESDAY, January 31

....
....
....
....
....

WEDNESDAY, February 1

....
....
....
....
....

THURSDAY, February 2

....
....
....
....
....

FRIDAY, February 3

....
....
....
....
....

SATURDAY, February 4

....
....
....
....
....

to-do list

- ☐ ....
- ☐ ....
- ☐ ....
- ☐ ....
- ☐ ....
- ☐ ....
- ☐ ....
- ☐ ....
- ☐ ....
- ☐ ....
- ☐ ....
- ☐ ....
- ☐ ....
- ☐ ....

"You don't have enough faith," Jesus told them. "I tell you the truth, if you had faith even as small as a mustard seed, you could say to this mountain, 'Move from here to there,' and it would move. Nothing would be impossible."
MATTHEW 17:20 NLT

February 2023

S	M	T	W	T	F	S
			1	2	3	4
5	6	7	8	9	10	11
12	13	14	15	16	17	18
19	20	21	22	23	24	25
26	27	28				

God hears your prayers.
Don't ever forget that!

to-do list

- ☐ ....
- ☐ ....
- ☐ ....
- ☐ ....
- ☐ ....
- ☐ ....
- ☐ ....
- ☐ ....
- ☐ ....
- ☐ ....
- ☐ ....
- ☐ ....
- ☐ ....
- ☐ ....
- ☐ ....
- ☐ ....
- ☐ ....
- ☐ ....

SUNDAY, February 5

....
....
....
....
....

MONDAY, February 6

....
....
....
....
....

TUESDAY, February 7

....
....
....
....
....

WEDNESDAY, February 8

....
....
....
....
....

THURSDAY, February 9

....
....
....
....
....

FRIDAY, February 10

....
....
....
....
....

SATURDAY, February 11

....
....
....
....
....

to-do list

- [ ] ....
- [ ] ....
- [ ] ....
- [ ] ....
- [ ] ....
- [ ] ....
- [ ] ....
- [ ] ....
- [ ] ....
- [ ] ....
- [ ] ....
- [ ] ....
- [ ] ....
- [ ] ....
- [ ] ....
- [ ] ....
- [ ] ....
- [ ] ....

The LORD is far from the wicked, but he hears the prayer of the righteous.
PROVERBS 15:29 ESV

February 2023

S	M	T	W	T	F	S
			1	2	3	4
5	6	7	8	9	10	11
12	13	14	15	16	17	18
19	20	21	22	23	24	25
26	27	28				

Abide in Christ. Hang out with Him.
Love on Him. You were born to abide.

to-do list

- [ ] ....
- [ ] ....
- [ ] ....
- [ ] ....
- [ ] ....
- [ ] ....
- [ ] ....
- [ ] ....
- [ ] ....
- [ ] ....
- [ ] ....
- [ ] ....
- [ ] ....
- [ ] ....
- [ ] ....
- [ ] ....
- [ ] ....
- [ ] ....

SUNDAY, February 12

....
....
....
....
....

MONDAY, February 13

....
....
....
....
....

TUESDAY, February 14   *Valentine's Day*

....
....
....
....
....

WEDNESDAY, February 15

....

....

....

....

....

THURSDAY, February 16

....

....

....

....

....

FRIDAY, February 17

....

....

....

....

....

SATURDAY, February 18

....

....

....

....

....

☐ ....

☐ ....

☐ ....

☐ ....

☐ ....

☐ ....

☐ ....

☐ ....

☐ ....

☐ ....

☐ ....

☐ ....

☐ ....

☐ ....

☐ ....

☐ ....

*"I am the vine; you
are the branches.
Whoever abides in
me and I in him, he
it is that bears much
fruit, for apart from me
you can do nothing."*
JOHN 15:5 ESV

February 2023

S	M	T	W	T	F	S
			1	2	3	4
5	6	7	8	9	10	11
12	13	14	15	16	17	18
19	20	21	22	23	24	25
26	27	28				

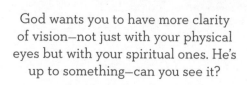

God wants you to have more clarity of vision—not just with your physical eyes but with your spiritual ones. He's up to something—can you see it?

to-do list

- [ ]
- [ ]
- [ ]
- [ ]
- [ ]
- [ ]
- [ ]
- [ ]
- [ ]
- [ ]
- [ ]
- [ ]
- [ ]
- [ ]
- [ ]
- [ ]
- [ ]
- [ ]
- [ ]

SUNDAY, February 19

MONDAY, February 20   *Presidents Day*

TUESDAY, February 21

WEDNESDAY, February 22 *Ash Wednesday*

....
....
....
....
....

THURSDAY, February 23

....
....
....
....
....

FRIDAY, February 24

....
....
....
....
....

SATURDAY, February 25

....
....
....
....
....

to-do list

☐ ....
☐ ....
☐ ....
☐ ....
☐ ....
☐ ....
☐ ....
☐ ....
☐ ....
☐ ....
☐ ....
☐ ....
☐ ....
☐ ....
☐ ....
☐ ....

Trust in the LORD with all your heart; do not depend on your own understanding. Seek his will in all you do, and he will show you which path to take.
PROVERBS 3:5-6 NLT

February–March 2023

S	M	T	W	T	F	S
			1	2	3	4
5	6	7	8	9	10	11
12	13	14	15	16	17	18
19	20	21	22	23	24	25
26	27	28				

God designed you to receive blessings,
sister. He has poured out many already,
but there are surprises yet to come.
Are you ready to receive them?

to-do list

☐ ....
☐ ....
☐ ....
☐ ....
☐ ....
☐ ....
☐ ....
☐ ....
☐ ....
☐ ....
☐ ....
☐ ....
☐ ....
☐ ....
☐ ....
☐ ....
☐ ....
☐ ....

SUNDAY, February 26

....
....
....
....
....

MONDAY, February 27

....
....
....
....
....

TUESDAY, February 28

....
....
....
....
....

WEDNESDAY, March 1

....
....
....
....
....

THURSDAY, March 2

....
....
....
....
....

FRIDAY, March 3

....
....
....
....
....

SATURDAY, March 4

....
....
....
....
....

to-do list

☐ ....
☐ ....
☐ ....
☐ ....
☐ ....
☐ ....
☐ ....
☐ ....
☐ ....
☐ ....
☐ ....
☐ ....
☐ ....
☐ ....
☐ ....
☐ ....

*The trustworthy person
will get a rich reward,
but a person who
wants quick riches
will get into trouble.*
PROVERBS 28:20 NLT

March  2023

SUNDAY	MONDAY	TUESDAY	WEDNESDAY
26	27	28	1
5	6	7	8
12 *Daylight Saving Time Begins*	13	14	15
19	20 *First Day of Spring*	21	22
26	27	28	29

notes

THURSDAY	FRIDAY	SATURDAY
2	3	4
9	10	11
16	17	18
	St. Patrick's Day	
23	24	25
30	31	1

....
....
....
....
....
....
....
....
....
....
....
....
....

FEBRUARY

S	M	T	W	T	F	S
			1	2	3	4
5	6	7	8	9	10	11
12	13	14	15	16	17	18
19	20	21	22	23	24	25
26	27	28				

APRIL

S	M	T	W	T	F	S
						1
2	3	4	5	6	7	8
9	10	11	12	13	14	15
16	17	18	19	20	21	22
23	24	25	26	27	28	29
30						

Don't ever stop asking for God's healing and strength.
What you cannot do on your own, He can surely do for you.

Goals *for* This Month

Be strong and courageous, all you who put your hope in the LORD!
PSALM 31:24 NLT

March 2023

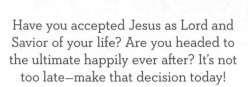

S	M	T	W	T	F	S
			1	2	3	4
5	6	7	8	9	10	11
12	13	14	15	16	17	18
19	20	21	22	23	24	25
26	27	28	29	30	31	

Have you accepted Jesus as Lord and Savior of your life? Are you headed to the ultimate happily ever after? It's not too late—make that decision today!

to-do list

☐ ....
☐ ....
☐ ....
☐ ....
☐ ....
☐ ....
☐ ....
☐ ....
☐ ....
☐ ....
☐ ....
☐ ....
☐ ....
☐ ....
☐ ....
☐ ....
☐ ....
☐ ....

SUNDAY, March 5

....
....
....
....
....

MONDAY, March 6

....
....
....
....
....

TUESDAY, March 7

....
....
....
....
....

WEDNESDAY, March 8

- ☐ ....
- ☐ ....
- ☐ ....
- ☐ ....
- ☐ ....

THURSDAY, March 9

- ☐ ....
- ☐ ....
- ☐ ....
- ☐ ....
- ☐ ....
- ☐ ....

FRIDAY, March 10

- ☐ ....
- ☐ ....
- ☐ ....

SATURDAY, March 11

Yet God has made everything beautiful for its own time. He has planted eternity in the human heart, but even so, people cannot see the whole scope of God's work from beginning to end.

ECCLESIASTES 3:11 NLT

March 2023

S	M	T	W	T	F	S
			1	2	3	4
5	6	7	8	9	10	11
12	13	14	15	16	17	18
19	20	21	22	23	24	25
26	27	28	29	30	31	

God longs to bring good from the bad in your life. You were created for more victory stories.

to-do list

☐ ....
☐ ....
☐ ....
☐ ....
☐ ....
☐ ....
☐ ....
☐ ....
☐ ....
☐ ....
☐ ....
☐ ....
☐ ....
☐ ....
☐ ....
☐ ....
☐ ....

SUNDAY, March 12 *Daylight Saving Time Begins*

....
....
....
....
....

MONDAY, March 13

....
....
....
....
....

TUESDAY, March 14

....
....
....
....
....

WEDNESDAY, March 15

....
....
....
....
....

THURSDAY, March 16

....
....
....
....
....

FRIDAY, March 17   *St. Patrick's Day*

....
....
....
....
....

SATURDAY, March 18

....
....
....
....

to-do list

☐ ....
☐ ....
☐ ....
☐ ....
☐ ....
☐ ....
☐ ....
☐ ....
☐ ....
☐ ....
☐ ....
☐ ....
☐ ....
☐ ....
☐ ....
☐ ....

*We know that God
makes all things work
together for the good
of those who love Him
and are chosen to be
a part of His plan.*
ROMANS 8:28 NLV

March 2023

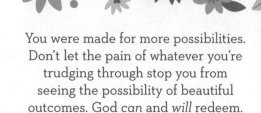

S	M	T	W	T	F	S
			1	2	3	4
5	6	7	8	9	10	11
12	13	14	15	16	17	18
19	20	21	22	23	24	25
26	27	28	29	30	31	

You were made for more possibilities. Don't let the pain of whatever you're trudging through stop you from seeing the possibility of beautiful outcomes. God *can* and *will* redeem.

to-do list

- [ ]
- [ ]
- [ ]
- [ ]
- [ ]
- [ ]
- [ ]
- [ ]
- [ ]
- [ ]
- [ ]
- [ ]
- [ ]
- [ ]
- [ ]
- [ ]
- [ ]
- [ ]
- [ ]

SUNDAY, March 19

MONDAY, March 20   *First Day of Spring*

TUESDAY, March 21

WEDNESDAY, March 22

....
....
....
....
....

THURSDAY, March 23

....
....
....
....
....

FRIDAY, March 24

....
....
....
....
....

SATURDAY, March 25

....
....
....
....
....

to-do list

☐ ....
☐ ....
☐ ....
☐ ....
☐ ....
☐ ....
☐ ....
☐ ....
☐ ....
☐ ....
☐ ....
☐ ....
☐ ....
☐ ....
☐ ....
☐ ....
☐ ....
☐ ....

Jesus looked at them and said, "This cannot be done by men. But with God all things can be done."
MATTHEW 19:26 NLV

March–April 2023

S	M	T	W	T	F	S
			1	2	3	4
5	6	7	8	9	10	11
12	13	14	15	16	17	18
19	20	21	22	23	24	25
26	27	28	29	30	31	

Ask God to show you how to overcome your lack of confidence when it strikes, and then turn your gaze to Him. He's the confidence booster, the One you can trust for a heavenly boost.

to-do list

- [ ] ....
- [ ] ....
- [ ] ....
- [ ] ....
- [ ] ....
- [ ] ....
- [ ] ....
- [ ] ....
- [ ] ....
- [ ] ....
- [ ] ....
- [ ] ....
- [ ] ....
- [ ] ....
- [ ] ....
- [ ] ....
- [ ] ....
- [ ] ....

SUNDAY, March 26

....
....
....
....
....

MONDAY, March 27

....
....
....
....
....

TUESDAY, March 28

....
....
....
....
....

WEDNESDAY, March 29

THURSDAY, March 30

FRIDAY, March 31

SATURDAY, April 1

to-do list

- [ ]
- [ ]
- [ ]
- [ ]
- [ ]
- [ ]
- [ ]
- [ ]
- [ ]
- [ ]
- [ ]
- [ ]
- [ ]
- [ ]
- [ ]
- [ ]
- [ ]

*Let us then with
confidence draw near
to the throne of grace,
that we may receive
mercy and find grace
to help in time of need.*
HEBREWS 4:16 ESV

April 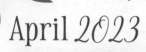 2023

SUNDAY	MONDAY	TUESDAY	WEDNESDAY
26	27	28	29
2 *Palm Sunday*	3	4	5 *Passover Begins at Sundown*
9 *Easter*	10	11	12
16	17	18	19
23 30	24	25	26

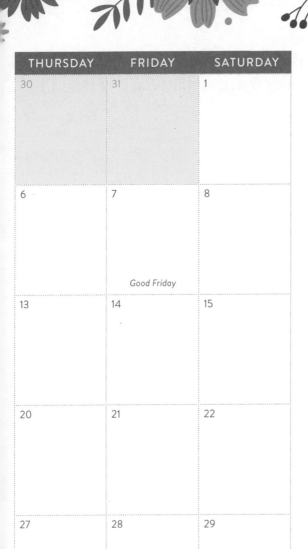

notes

THURSDAY	FRIDAY	SATURDAY
30	31	1
6	7 *Good Friday*	8
13	14	15
20	21	22
27	28	29

MARCH

S	M	T	W	T	F	S
			1	2	3	4
5	6	7	8	9	10	11
12	13	14	15	16	17	18
19	20	21	22	23	24	25
26	27	28	29	30	31	

MAY

S	M	T	W	T	F	S
	1	2	3	4	5	6
7	8	9	10	11	12	13
14	15	16	17	18	19	20
21	22	23	24	25	26	27
28	29	30	31			

You are made righteous–*worthy*–because of the blood of Jesus. It's true! You're worthy because of Him.

Goals *for* This Month

*To this end we always pray for you, that our God may
make you worthy of his calling and may fulfill every
resolve for good and every work of faith by his power.*
2 THESSALONIANS 1:11 ESV

April 2023

S	M	T	W	T	F	S
						1
2	3	4	5	6	7	8
9	10	11	12	13	14	15
16	17	18	19	20	21	22
23	24	25	26	27	28	29
30						

God wants you to overflow, to spill out onto others. Spill out what, exactly? Love. Joy. Peace. Long-suffering. Goodness. Patience.

to-do list

- [ ]
- [ ]
- [ ]
- [ ]
- [ ]
- [ ]
- [ ]
- [ ]
- [ ]
- [ ]
- [ ]
- [ ]
- [ ]
- [ ]
- [ ]
- [ ]
- [ ]
- [ ]

SUNDAY, April 2   *Palm Sunday*

....

....

....

....

....

MONDAY, April 3

....

....

....

....

....

TUESDAY, April 4

....

....

....

....

....

WEDNESDAY, April 5   *Passover Begins at Sundown*

....

....

....

....

....

THURSDAY, April 6

....

....

....

....

....

FRIDAY, April 7   *Good Friday*

....

....

....

....

SATURDAY, April 8

....

....

....

....

....

to-do list

☐ ....
☐ ....
☐ ....
☐ ....
☐ ....
☐ ....
☐ ....
☐ ....
☐ ....
☐ ....
☐ ....
☐ ....
☐ ....
☐ ....
☐ ....

*Our hope comes from
God. May He fill you
with joy and peace
because of your trust
in Him. May your hope
grow stronger by the
power of the Holy Spirit.*
ROMANS 15:13 NLV

April 2023

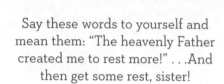

S	M	T	W	T	F	S
						1
2	3	4	5	6	7	8
9	10	11	12	13	14	15
16	17	18	19	20	21	22
23	24	25	26	27	28	29
30						

Say these words to yourself and mean them: "The heavenly Father created me to rest more!" . . .And then get some rest, sister!

to-do list

- [ ]
- [ ]
- [ ]
- [ ]
- [ ]
- [ ]
- [ ]
- [ ]
- [ ]
- [ ]
- [ ]
- [ ]
- [ ]
- [ ]
- [ ]
- [ ]
- [ ]
- [ ]

SUNDAY, April 9   *Easter*

MONDAY, April 10

TUESDAY, April 11

WEDNESDAY, April 12

- [ ] ....
- [ ] ....
- [ ] ....
- [ ] ....
- [ ] ....
- [ ] ....

THURSDAY, April 13

- [ ] ....
- [ ] ....
- [ ] ....
- [ ] ....
- [ ] ....
- [ ] ....

FRIDAY, April 14

- [ ] ....
- [ ] ....
- [ ] ....
- [ ] ....

SATURDAY, April 15

"Come to me, all you who are weary and burdened, and I will give you rest."
MATTHEW 11:28 NIV

April 2023

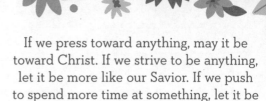

S	M	T	W	T	F	S
						1
2	3	4	5	6	7	8
9	10	11	12	13	14	15
16	17	18	19	20	21	22
23	24	25	26	27	28	29
30						

If we press toward anything, may it be toward Christ. If we strive to be anything, let it be more like our Savior. If we push to spend more time at something, let it be at developing our prayer and worship life.

to-do list

- [ ]
- [ ]
- [ ]
- [ ]
- [ ]
- [ ]
- [ ]
- [ ]
- [ ]
- [ ]
- [ ]
- [ ]
- [ ]
- [ ]
- [ ]
- [ ]
- [ ]
- [ ]
- [ ]

SUNDAY, April 16

MONDAY, April 17

TUESDAY, April 18

WEDNESDAY, April 19

THURSDAY, April 20

FRIDAY, April 21

SATURDAY, April 22

to-do list

☐ ....
☐ ....
☐ ....
☐ ....
☐ ....
☐ ....
☐ ....
☐ ....
☐ ....
☐ ....
☐ ....
☐ ....
☐ ....
☐ ....
☐ ....
☐ ....

*Not that I have already
obtained this or am
already perfect, but
I press on to make
it my own, because
Christ Jesus has
made me his own.*
PHILIPPIANS 3:12 ESV

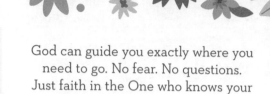

April 2023

S	M	T	W	T	F	S
						1
2	3	4	5	6	7	8
9	10	11	12	13	14	15
16	17	18	19	20	21	22
23	24	25	26	27	28	29
30						

God can guide you exactly where you need to go. No fear. No questions. Just faith in the One who knows your path better than you ever could.

to-do list

- [ ]
- [ ]
- [ ]
- [ ]
- [ ]
- [ ]
- [ ]
- [ ]
- [ ]
- [ ]
- [ ]
- [ ]
- [ ]
- [ ]
- [ ]
- [ ]
- [ ]
- [ ]

SUNDAY, April 23

MONDAY, April 24

TUESDAY, April 25

WEDNESDAY, April 26

....
....
....
....
....

THURSDAY, April 27

....
....
....
....
....

FRIDAY, April 28

....
....
....
....
....

SATURDAY, April 29

....
....
....
....
....

to-do list

☐ ....
☐ ....
☐ ....
☐ ....
☐ ....
☐ ....
☐ ....
☐ ....
☐ ....
☐ ....
☐ ....
☐ ....
☐ ....
☐ ....
☐ ....
☐ ....

*For we walk by
faith, not by sight.*
2 CORINTHIANS 5:7 ESV

May 2023

SUNDAY	MONDAY	TUESDAY	WEDNESDAY
30	1	2	3
7	8	9	10
14 *Mother's Day*	15	16	17
21	22	23	24
28	29 *Memorial Day*	30	31

notes

THURSDAY	FRIDAY	SATURDAY
4 *National Day of Prayer*	5	6
11	12	13
18	19	20
25	26	27
1	2	3

....
....
....
....
....
....
....
....
....
....
....
....

APRIL

S	M	T	W	T	F	S
						1
2	3	4	5	6	7	8
9	10	11	12	13	14	15
16	17	18	19	20	21	22
23	24	25	26	27	28	29
30						

JUNE

S	M	T	W	T	F	S
				1	2	3
4	5	6	7	8	9	10
11	12	13	14	15	16	17
18	19	20	21	22	23	24
25	26	27	28	29	30	

You were created to succeed. Think about that for a moment. The God of the universe wants you—yes, *you!*—to accomplish great and mighty things.

Goals *for* This Month

*May he give you the desire of your heart
and make all your plans succeed.*

PSALM 20:4 NIV

April–May 2023

S	M	T	W	T	F	S
						1	2	3	4	5	6
7	8	9	10	11	12	13
14	15	16	17	18	19	20
21	22	23	24	25	26	27
28	29	30	31			

Open your eyes and your heart! God is going to use you to be generous in ways you never dreamed possible.

to-do list

- [ ]
- [ ]
- [ ]
- [ ]
- [ ]
- [ ]
- [ ]
- [ ]
- [ ]
- [ ]
- [ ]
- [ ]
- [ ]
- [ ]
- [ ]
- [ ]
- [ ]
- [ ]

SUNDAY, April 30

MONDAY, May 1

TUESDAY, May 2

WEDNESDAY, May 3

....
....
....
....
....

THURSDAY, May 4   *National Day of Prayer*

....
....
....
....
....

FRIDAY, May 5

....
....
....
....
....

SATURDAY, May 6

....
....
....
....
....

to-do list

☐ ....
☐ ....
☐ ....
☐ ....
☐ ....
☐ ....
☐ ....
☐ ....
☐ ....
☐ ....
☐ ....
☐ ....
☐ ....
☐ ....
☐ ....

"But who am I, and who are my people, that we should be able to give as generously as this? Everything comes from you, and we have given you only what comes from your hand."

1 CHRONICLES 29:14 NIV

May 2023

S	M	T	W	T	F	S
	1	2	3	4	5	6
7	8	9	10	11	12	13
14	15	16	17	18	19	20
21	22	23	24	25	26	27
28	29	30	31			

The heavenly Father adores you! You were made for more time gazing at Him.

to-do list

☐ ....
☐ ....
☐ ....
☐ ....
☐ ....
☐ ....
☐ ....
☐ ....
☐ ....
☐ ....
☐ ....
☐ ....
☐ ....
☐ ....
☐ ....
☐ ....
☐ ....
☐ ....

SUNDAY, May 7

....
....
....
....
....

MONDAY, May 8

....
....
....
....
....

TUESDAY, May 9

....
....
....
....
....

WEDNESDAY, May 10

....

....

....

....

....

THURSDAY, May 11

....

....

....

....

....

FRIDAY, May 12

....

....

....

....

....

SATURDAY, May 13

....

....

....

....

....

to-do list

☐ ....

☐ ....

☐ ....

☐ ....

☐ ....

☐ ....

☐ ....

☐ ....

☐ ....

☐ ....

☐ ....

☐ ....

☐ ....

☐ ....

☐ ....

*One thing I have asked
from the Lord, that I will
look for: that I may live
in the house of the Lord
all the days of my life, to
look upon the beauty of
the Lord, and to worship
in His holy house.*
PSALM 27:4 NLV

May 2023

S	M	T	W	T	F	S
	1	2	3	4	5	6
7	8	9	10	11	12	13
14	15	16	17	18	19	20
21	22	23	24	25	26	27
28	29	30	31			

God can give you the "oomph" to make it through, even when you're completely convinced you can't. Just ask Him!

to-do list

- [ ] ....
- [ ] ....
- [ ] ....
- [ ] ....
- [ ] ....
- [ ] ....
- [ ] ....
- [ ] ....
- [ ] ....
- [ ] ....
- [ ] ....
- [ ] ....
- [ ] ....
- [ ] ....
- [ ] ....
- [ ] ....
- [ ] ....
- [ ] ....
- [ ] ....

SUNDAY, May 14 *Mother's Day*

....
....
....
....
....

MONDAY, May 15

....
....
....
....
....

TUESDAY, May 16

....
....
....
....
....

WEDNESDAY, May 17

....
....
....
....
....

THURSDAY, May 18

....
....
....
....
....

FRIDAY, May 19

....
....
....
....
....

SATURDAY, May 20

....
....
....
....
....

to-do list

☐ ....
☐ ....
☐ ....
☐ ....
☐ ....
☐ ....
☐ ....
☐ ....
☐ ....
☐ ....
☐ ....
☐ ....
☐ ....
☐ ....
☐ ....
☐ ....

*My flesh and my heart
may fail, but God is the
strength of my heart
and my portion forever.*
PSALM 73:26 NIV

May 2023

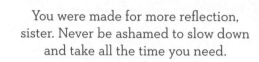

S	M	T	W	T	F	S
	1	2	3	4	5	6
7	8	9	10	11	12	13
14	15	16	17	18	19	20
21	22	23	24	25	26	27
28	29	30	31			

You were made for more reflection, sister. Never be ashamed to slow down and take all the time you need.

to-do list

- ☐ ....
- ☐ ....
- ☐ ....
- ☐ ....
- ☐ ....
- ☐ ....
- ☐ ....
- ☐ ....
- ☐ ....
- ☐ ....
- ☐ ....
- ☐ ....
- ☐ ....
- ☐ ....
- ☐ ....
- ☐ ....
- ☐ ....
- ☐ ....

SUNDAY, May 21

....
....
....
....
....

MONDAY, May 22

....
....
....
....
....

TUESDAY, May 23

....
....
....
....
....

WEDNESDAY, May 24

....
....
....
....
....

THURSDAY, May 25

....
....
....
....
....

FRIDAY, May 26

....
....
....
....
....

SATURDAY, May 27

....
....
....
....

to-do list

- [ ] ....
- [ ] ....
- [ ] ....
- [ ] ....
- [ ] ....
- [ ] ....
- [ ] ....
- [ ] ....
- [ ] ....
- [ ] ....
- [ ] ....
- [ ] ....
- [ ] ....
- [ ] ....

Now that which we see is as if we were looking in a broken mirror. But then we will see everything. Now I know only a part. But then I will know everything in a perfect way. That is how God knows me right now.
1 CORINTHIANS 13:12 NLV

May–June 2023

S	M	T	W	T	F	S
	1	2	3	4	5	6
7	8	9	10	11	12	13
14	15	16	17	18	19	20
21	22	23	24	25	26	27
28	29	30	31			

You were designed to encourage more, love more, and build up others in good times and bad.

to-do list

- [ ] ....
- [ ] ....
- [ ] ....
- [ ] ....
- [ ] ....
- [ ] ....
- [ ] ....
- [ ] ....
- [ ] ....
- [ ] ....
- [ ] ....
- [ ] ....
- [ ] ....
- [ ] ....
- [ ] ....
- [ ] ....
- [ ] ....
- [ ] ....

SUNDAY, May 28

....
....
....
....
....

MONDAY, May 29   *Memorial Day*

....
....
....
....
....

TUESDAY, May 30

....
....
....
....
....

WEDNESDAY, May 31

THURSDAY, June 1

FRIDAY, June 2

SATURDAY, June 3

to-do list

☐ ....
☐ ....
☐ ....
☐ ....
☐ ....
☐ ....
☐ ....
☐ ....
☐ ....
☐ ....
☐ ....
☐ ....
☐ ....
☐ ....
☐ ....
☐ ....
☐ ....

Therefore encourage one another and build each other up, just as in fact you are doing.
1 THESSALONIANS 5:11 NIV

June 2023

SUNDAY	MONDAY	TUESDAY	WEDNESDAY
28	29	30	31
4	5	6	7
11	12	13	14 *Flag Day*
18 *Father's Day*	19	20	21 *First Day of Summer*
25	26	27	28

notes

THURSDAY	FRIDAY	SATURDAY
1	2	3
8	9	10
15	16	17
22	23	24
29	30	1

....
....
....
....
....
....
....
....
....
....
....
....
....
....

MAY

S	M	T	W	T	F	S
	1	2	3	4	5	6
7	8	9	10	11	12	13
14	15	16	17	18	19	20
21	22	23	24	25	26	27
28	29	30	31			

JULY

S	M	T	W	T	F	S
						1
2	3	4	5	6	7	8
9	10	11	12	13	14	15
16	17	18	19	20	21	22
23	24	25	26	27	28	29
30	31					

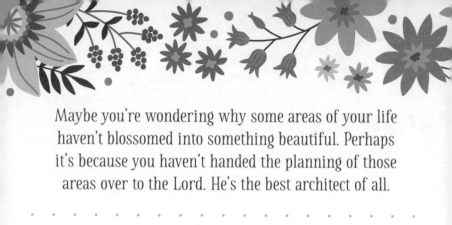

Maybe you're wondering why some areas of your life haven't blossomed into something beautiful. Perhaps it's because you haven't handed the planning of those areas over to the Lord. He's the best architect of all.

Goals *for* This Month

*Commit to the LORD whatever you do,
and he will establish your plans.*

PROVERBS 16:3 NIV

June 2023

S	M	T	W	T	F	S
				1	2	3
4	5	6	7	8	9	10
11	12	13	14	15	16	17
18	19	20	21	22	23	24
25	26	27	28	29	30	

When you're in relationship with Christ—when you place your love for Him above all else—then your desires fall into alignment with what He wants for your life.

to-do list

- [ ]
- [ ]
- [ ]
- [ ]
- [ ]
- [ ]
- [ ]
- [ ]
- [ ]
- [ ]
- [ ]
- [ ]
- [ ]
- [ ]
- [ ]
- [ ]
- [ ]
- [ ]

SUNDAY, June 4

MONDAY, June 5

TUESDAY, June 6

WEDNESDAY, June 7

....
....
....
....
....

THURSDAY, June 8

....
....
....
....
....

FRIDAY, June 9

....
....
....
....
....

SATURDAY, June 10

....
....
....
....
....

to-do list

- [ ] ....
- [ ] ....
- [ ] ....
- [ ] ....
- [ ] ....
- [ ] ....
- [ ] ....
- [ ] ....
- [ ] ....
- [ ] ....
- [ ] ....
- [ ] ....
- [ ] ....
- [ ] ....
- [ ] ....
- [ ] ....
- [ ] ....

*Be happy in the Lord.
And He will give you the
desires of your heart.*
PSALM 37:4 NLV

June 2023

S	M	T	W	T	F	S
				1	2	3
4	5	6	7	8	9	10
11	12	13	14	15	16	17
18	19	20	21	22	23	24
25	26	27	28	29	30	

Are you feeling the power of the Spirit today? If not, ask for it! The more you ask the Spirit of God to fill you, the stronger you'll be.

to-do list

- [ ]
- [ ]
- [ ]
- [ ]
- [ ]
- [ ]
- [ ]
- [ ]
- [ ]
- [ ]
- [ ]
- [ ]
- [ ]
- [ ]
- [ ]
- [ ]
- [ ]
- [ ]

SUNDAY, June 11

MONDAY, June 12

TUESDAY, June 13

WEDNESDAY, June 14 *Flag Day*

....
....
....
....
....

THURSDAY, June 15

....
....
....
....
....

FRIDAY, June 16

....
....
....
....
....

SATURDAY, June 17

....
....
....
....
....

to-do list

- [ ] ....
- [ ] ....
- [ ] ....
- [ ] ....
- [ ] ....
- [ ] ....
- [ ] ....
- [ ] ....
- [ ] ....
- [ ] ....
- [ ] ....
- [ ] ....
- [ ] ....
- [ ] ....
- [ ] ....
- [ ] ....

*May the God of hope
fill you with all joy and
peace as you trust
in him, so that you
may overflow with
hope by the power
of the Holy Spirit.*
ROMANS 15:13 NIV

June 2023

S	M	T	W	T	F	S
				1	2	3
4	5	6	7	8	9	10
11	12	13	14	15	16	17
18	19	20	21	22	23	24
25	26	27	28	29	30	

God created us with a destination in mind. He puts us on paths and guides us to where we need to go.

to-do list

- [ ]
- [ ]
- [ ]
- [ ]
- [ ]
- [ ]
- [ ]
- [ ]
- [ ]
- [ ]
- [ ]
- [ ]
- [ ]
- [ ]
- [ ]
- [ ]
- [ ]
- [ ]
- [ ]

SUNDAY, June 18 *Father's Day*

MONDAY, June 19

TUESDAY, June 20

WEDNESDAY, June 21   *First Day of Summer*

....
....
....
....
....

THURSDAY, June 22

....
....
....
....
....

FRIDAY, June 23

....
....
....
....
....

SATURDAY, June 24

....
....
....
....
....

to-do list

☐ ....
☐ ....
☐ ....
☐ ....
☐ ....
☐ ....
☐ ....
☐ ....
☐ ....
☐ ....
☐ ....
☐ ....
☐ ....
☐ ....
☐ ....
☐ ....
☐ ....

*He refreshes my soul.
He guides me along
the right paths for
his name's sake.*
PSALM 23:3 NIV

June–July 2023

S	M	T	W	T	F	S
				1	2	3
4	5	6	7	8	9	10
11	12	13	14	15	16	17
18	19	20	21	22	23	24
25	26	27	28	29	30	

One of the Lord's greatest desires is to lavish His children with unexpected treasures and joys. So don't be surprised when He goes exceedingly, abundantly above all you could ask or think.

to-do list

- [ ] ....
- [ ] ....
- [ ] ....
- [ ] ....
- [ ] ....
- [ ] ....
- [ ] ....
- [ ] ....
- [ ] ....
- [ ] ....
- [ ] ....
- [ ] ....
- [ ] ....
- [ ] ....
- [ ] ....
- [ ] ....
- [ ] ....

SUNDAY, June 25

....

....

....

....

....

MONDAY, June 26

....

....

....

....

....

TUESDAY, June 27

....

....

....

....

....

WEDNESDAY, June 28

THURSDAY, June 29

FRIDAY, June 30

SATURDAY, July 1

- [ ]
- [ ]
- [ ]
- [ ]
- [ ]
- [ ]
- [ ]
- [ ]
- [ ]
- [ ]
- [ ]
- [ ]
- [ ]

Now to him who is able to do immeasurably more than all we ask or imagine, according to his power that is at work within us, to him be glory in the church and in Christ Jesus throughout all generations, for ever and ever! Amen.
EPHESIANS 3:20-21 NIV

July

SUNDAY	MONDAY	TUESDAY	WEDNESDAY
25	26	27	28
2	3	4 *Independence Day*	5
9	10	11	12
16	17	18	19
23	24	25	26
30	31		

THURSDAY	FRIDAY	SATURDAY
29	30	1
6	7	8
13	14	15
20	21	22
27	28	29

notes

....
....
....
....
....
....
....
....
....
....
....
....
....

JUNE

S	M	T	W	T	F	S
				1	2	3
4	5	6	7	8	9	10
11	12	13	14	15	16	17
18	19	20	21	22	23	24
25	26	27	28	29	30	

AUGUST

S	M	T	W	T	F	S
		1	2	3	4	5
6	7	8	9	10	11	12
13	14	15	16	17	18	19
20	21	22	23	24	25	26
27	28	29	30	31		

Life is filled with challenges, but perhaps these seasons are when we're best able to see God's hand at work. In the deep waters, His promise remains: you will not drown. When the flames lap at you, the heat in your face more than you can stand, still He whispers, *"You will not be burned."*

Goals *for* This Month

"When you pass through the waters, I will be with you;
and when you pass through the rivers, they will not sweep
over you. When you walk through the fire, you will not
be burned; the flames will not set you ablaze."

ISAIAH 43:2 NIV

July 2023

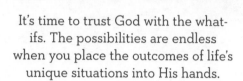

S	M	T	W	T	F	S
						1
2	3	4	5	6	7	8
9	10	11	12	13	14	15
16	17	18	19	20	21	22
23	24	25	26	27	28	29
30	31					

It's time to trust God with the what-ifs. The possibilities are endless when you place the outcomes of life's unique situations into His hands.

to-do list

- [ ]
- [ ]
- [ ]
- [ ]
- [ ]
- [ ]
- [ ]
- [ ]
- [ ]
- [ ]
- [ ]
- [ ]
- [ ]
- [ ]
- [ ]
- [ ]
- [ ]
- [ ]
- [ ]

SUNDAY, July 2

MONDAY, July 3

TUESDAY, July 4 *Independence Day*

WEDNESDAY, July 5

THURSDAY, July 6

FRIDAY, July 7

SATURDAY, July 8

to-do list

- [ ] ....
- [ ] ....
- [ ] ....
- [ ] ....
- [ ] ....
- [ ] ....
- [ ] ....
- [ ] ....
- [ ] ....
- [ ] ....
- [ ] ....
- [ ] ....
- [ ] ....
- [ ] ....
- [ ] ....
- [ ] ....
- [ ] ....

*"What do you mean,
'If I can'?" Jesus asked.
"Anything is possible
if a person believes."*
MARK 9:23 NLT

July 2023

S	M	T	W	T	F	S
						1
2	3	4	5	6	7	8
9	10	11	12	13	14	15
16	17	18	19	20	21	22
23	24	25	26	27	28	29
30	31					

Be careful how you live. Make the most of every opportunity. Why? Because the world is watching—people are looking to you to lead by example.

to-do list

- ☐
- ☐
- ☐
- ☐
- ☐
- ☐
- ☐
- ☐
- ☐
- ☐
- ☐
- ☐
- ☐
- ☐
- ☐
- ☐
- ☐
- ☐
- ☐

SUNDAY, July 9

MONDAY, July 10

TUESDAY, July 11

WEDNESDAY, July 12

THURSDAY, July 13

FRIDAY, July 14

SATURDAY, July 15

☐ ....
☐ ....
☐ ....
☐ ....
☐ ....
☐ ....
☐ ....
☐ ....
☐ ....
☐ ....
☐ ....
☐ ....
☐ ....
☐ ....
☐ ....
☐ ....

*Be very careful,
then, how you live—
not as unwise but
as wise, making
the most of every
opportunity, because
the days are evil.*
EPHESIANS 5:15-16 NIV

July 2023

S	M	T	W	T	F	S
						1
2	3	4	5	6	7	8
9	10	11	12	13	14	15
16	17	18	19	20	21	22
23	24	25	26	27	28	29
30	31					

You weren't created for chains—you were made for more than that. God created you to be set free from all the things that seek to bind you.

to-do list·

- [ ]
- [ ]
- [ ]
- [ ]
- [ ]
- [ ]
- [ ]
- [ ]
- [ ]
- [ ]
- [ ]
- [ ]
- [ ]
- [ ]
- [ ]
- [ ]
- [ ]
- [ ]

SUNDAY, July 16

MONDAY, July 17

TUESDAY, July 18

WEDNESDAY, July 19

☐ ....
☐ ....
☐ ....
☐ ....
☐ ....
☐ ....

THURSDAY, July 20

☐ ....
☐ ....
☐ ....
☐ ....
☐ ....
☐ ....

FRIDAY, July 21

☐ ....
☐ ....
☐ ....
☐ ....

SATURDAY, July 22

*About midnight
Paul and Silas were
praying and singing
hymns to God, and the
other prisoners were
listening to them.*
ACTS 16:25 NIV

July 2023

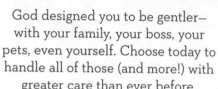

S	M	T	W	T	F	S
						1
2	3	4	5	6	7	8
9	10	11	12	13	14	15
16	17	18	19	20	21	22
23	24	25	26	27	28	29
30	31					

God designed you to be gentler—
with your family, your boss, your
pets, even yourself. Choose today to
handle all of those (and more!) with
greater care than ever before.

to-do list

- [ ] ....
- [ ] ....
- [ ] ....
- [ ] ....
- [ ] ....
- [ ] ....
- [ ] ....
- [ ] ....
- [ ] ....
- [ ] ....
- [ ] ....
- [ ] ....
- [ ] ....
- [ ] ....
- [ ] ....
- [ ] ....
- [ ] ....
- [ ] ....

SUNDAY, July 23

MONDAY, July 24

TUESDAY, July 25

WEDNESDAY, July 26

....
....
....
....
....

THURSDAY, July 27

....
....
....
....
....

FRIDAY, July 28

....
....
....
....
....

SATURDAY, July 29

....
....
....
....
....

to-do list

☐ ....
☐ ....
☐ ....
☐ ....
☐ ....
☐ ....
☐ ....
☐ ....
☐ ....
☐ ....
☐ ....
☐ ....
☐ ....
☐ ....
☐ ....

*But the Holy Spirit
produces this kind
of fruit in our lives:
love, joy, peace,
patience, kindness,
goodness, faithfulness,
gentleness, and self-
control. There is no law
against these things!*
GALATIANS 5:22–23 NLT

August 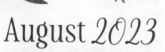 2023

SUNDAY	MONDAY	TUESDAY	WEDNESDAY
30	31	1	2
6	7	8	9
13	14	15	16
20	21	22	23
27	28	29	30

notes

THURSDAY	FRIDAY	SATURDAY
3	4	5
10	11	12
17	18	19
24	25	26
31	1	2

....
....
....
....
....
....
....
....
....
....
....
....

JULY

S	M	T	W	T	F	S
						1
2	3	4	5	6	7	8
9	10	11	12	13	14	15
16	17	18	19	20	21	22
23	24	25	26	27	28	29
30	31					

SEPTEMBER

S	M	T	W	T	F	S
					1	2
3	4	5	6	7	8	9
10	11	12	13	14	15	16
17	18	19	20	21	22	23
24	25	26	27	28	29	30

When it comes to blessings, God loves to
surprise His kids. So keep your eyes open!
He's sure to delight you with even more.

Goals *for* This Month

You prepare a table before me in the presence of my enemies; you anoint my head with oil; my cup overflows.
PSALM 23:5 ESV

July–August 2023

S	M	T	W	T	F	S
			1	2	3	4	5
6	7	8	9	10	11	12
13	14	15	16	17	18	19
20	21	22	23	24	25	26
27	28	29	30	31		

Don't conform to the world;
be transformed into Christ's image.
Change your mind. Make it more like His.

to-do list

☐ ....
☐ ....
☐ ....
☐ ....
☐ ....
☐ ....
☐ ....
☐ ....
☐ ....
☐ ....
☐ ....
☐ ....
☐ ....
☐ ....
☐ ....
☐ ....
☐ ....
☐ ....

SUNDAY, July 30

MONDAY, July 31

TUESDAY, August 1

WEDNESDAY, August 2

....

....

....

....

....

THURSDAY, August 3

....

....

....

....

....

FRIDAY, August 4

....

....

....

....

....

SATURDAY, August 5

....

....

....

....

....

to-do list

- [ ] ....
- [ ] ....
- [ ] ....
- [ ] ....
- [ ] ....
- [ ] ....
- [ ] ....
- [ ] ....
- [ ] ....
- [ ] ....
- [ ] ....
- [ ] ....
- [ ] ....
- [ ] ....

Do not conform to the pattern of this world, but be transformed by the renewing of your mind. Then you will be able to test and approve what God's will is—his good, pleasing and perfect will.
ROMANS 12:2 NIV

August 2023

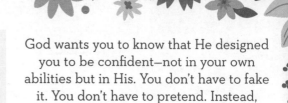

S	M	T	W	T	F	S
		1	2	3	4	5
6	7	8	9	10	11	12
13	14	15	16	17	18	19
20	21	22	23	24	25	26
27	28	29	30	31		

God wants you to know that He designed you to be confident—not in your own abilities but in His. You don't have to fake it. You don't have to pretend. Instead, seek the real deal in Jesus Christ.

to-do list

- ☐ ....
- ☐ ....
- ☐ ....
- ☐ ....
- ☐ ....
- ☐ ....
- ☐ ....
- ☐ ....
- ☐ ....
- ☐ ....
- ☐ ....
- ☐ ....
- ☐ ....
- ☐ ....
- ☐ ....
- ☐ ....
- ☐ ....
- ☐ ....

SUNDAY, August 6

....

....

....

....

....

MONDAY, August 7

....

....

....

....

....

TUESDAY, August 8

....

....

....

....

....

WEDNESDAY, August 9

....
....
....
....
....

THURSDAY, August 10

....
....
....
....
....

FRIDAY, August 11

....
....
....
....
....

SATURDAY, August 12

....
....
....
....
....

to-do list

- [ ] ....
- [ ] ....
- [ ] ....
- [ ] ....
- [ ] ....
- [ ] ....
- [ ] ....
- [ ] ....
- [ ] ....
- [ ] ....
- [ ] ....
- [ ] ....
- [ ] ....
- [ ] ....
- [ ] ....
- [ ] ....

*Let us then approach
God's throne of grace
with confidence, so that
we may receive mercy
and find grace to help
us in our time of need.*
HEBREWS 4:16 NIV

August 2023

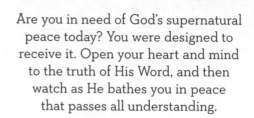

S	M	T	W	T	F	S
		1	2	3	4	5
6	7	8	9	10	11	12
13	14	15	16	17	18	19
20	21	22	23	24	25	26
27	28	29	30	31		

Are you in need of God's supernatural peace today? You were designed to receive it. Open your heart and mind to the truth of His Word, and then watch as He bathes you in peace that passes all understanding.

to-do list

☐ ....
☐ ....
☐ ....
☐ ....
☐ ....
☐ ....
☐ ....
☐ ....
☐ ....
☐ ....
☐ ....
☐ ....
☐ ....
☐ ....
☐ ....
☐ ....
☐ ....
☐ ....
☐ ....

SUNDAY, August 13

....
....
....
....
....

MONDAY, August 14

....
....
....
....
....

TUESDAY, August 15

....
....
....
....
....

WEDNESDAY, August 16

....
....
....
....
....

THURSDAY, August 17

....
....
....
....
....

FRIDAY, August 18

....
....
....
....
....

SATURDAY, August 19

....
....
....
....
....

to-do list

- [ ] ....
- [ ] ....
- [ ] ....
- [ ] ....
- [ ] ....
- [ ] ....
- [ ] ....
- [ ] ....
- [ ] ....
- [ ] ....
- [ ] ....
- [ ] ....
- [ ] ....
- [ ] ....
- [ ] ....
- [ ] ....
- [ ] ....

*And the peace of God,
which transcends all
understanding, will
guard your hearts
and your minds in
Christ Jesus.*
PHILIPPIANS 4:7 NIV

August 2023

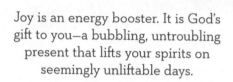

S	M	T	W	T	F	S
		1	2	3	4	5
6	7	8	9	10	11	12
13	14	15	16	17	18	19
20	21	22	23	24	25	26
27	28	29	30	31		

Joy is an energy booster. It is God's gift to you—a bubbling, untroubling present that lifts your spirits on seemingly unliftable days.

to-do list

☐ ....
☐ ....
☐ ....
☐ ....
☐ ....
☐ ....
☐ ....
☐ ....
☐ ....
☐ ....
☐ ....
☐ ....
☐ ....
☐ ....
☐ ....
☐ ....
☐ ....
☐ ....

SUNDAY, August 20

....
....
....
....
....

MONDAY, August 21

....
....
....
....
....

TUESDAY, August 22

....
....
....
....
....

WEDNESDAY, August 23

☐ ....
☐ ....
☐ ....
☐ ....
☐ ....
☐ ....

THURSDAY, August 24

☐ ....
☐ ....
☐ ....
☐ ....
☐ ....
☐ ....
☐ ....

FRIDAY, August 25

☐ ....
☐ ....
☐ ....
☐ ....

SATURDAY, August 26

*The LORD is my strength
and shield. I trust him
with all my heart. He
helps me, and my
heart is filled with joy.
I burst out in songs
of thanksgiving.*
PSALM 28:7 NLT

August–September 2023

S	M	T	W	T	F	S
		1	2	3	4	5
6	7	8	9	10	11	12
13	14	15	16	17	18	19
20	21	22	23	24	25	26
27	28	29	30	31		

You were created for more of the heavenly Father's covering, more of His protection. Lean on Him today, no matter what you're going through. He won't let you down.

to-do list

☐ ....
☐ ....
☐ ....
☐ ....
☐ ....
☐ ....
☐ ....
☐ ....
☐ ....
☐ ....
☐ ....
☐ ....
☐ ....
☐ ....
☐ ....
☐ ....
☐ ....
☐ ....

SUNDAY, August 27

....
....
....
....
....

MONDAY, August 28

....
....
....
....
....

TUESDAY, August 29

....
....
....
....
....

WEDNESDAY, August 30

....
....
....
....
....

THURSDAY, August 31

....
....
....
....
....

FRIDAY, September 1

....
....
....
....
....

SATURDAY, September 2

....
....
....
....
....

to-do list

- [ ] ....
- [ ] ....
- [ ] ....
- [ ] ....
- [ ] ....
- [ ] ....
- [ ] ....
- [ ] ....
- [ ] ....
- [ ] ....
- [ ] ....
- [ ] ....
- [ ] ....
- [ ] ....
- [ ] ....
- [ ] ....
- [ ] ....

*Though a thousand fall
at your side, though
ten thousand are dying
around you, these evils
will not touch you.*
PSALM 91:7 NLT

September 2023

SUNDAY	MONDAY	TUESDAY	WEDNESDAY
27	28	29	30
3	4 *Labor Day*	5	6
10	11	12	13
17	18	19	20
24	25	26	27

THURSDAY	FRIDAY	SATURDAY
31	1	2
7	8	9
14	15	16
21	22	23
		First Day of Autumn
28	29	30

notes

....
....
....
....
....
....
....
....
....
....
....
....
....
....

AUGUST

S	M	T	W	T	F	S
		1	2	3	4	5
6	7	8	9	10	11	12
13	14	15	16	17	18	19
20	21	22	23	24	25	26
27	28	29	30	31		

OCTOBER

S	M	T	W	T	F	S
1	2	3	4	5	6	7
8	9	10	11	12	13	14
15	16	17	18	19	20	21
22	23	24	25	26	27	28
29	30	31				

Hope is a propellant, a healer, an inspirer.
And hope is what our heavenly Father wants
us to have–*especially* in hopeless times.

Goals *for* This Month

May the God of hope fill you with all joy and peace in believing,
so that by the power of the Holy Spirit you may abound in hope.

ROMANS 15:13 ESV

September 2023

S	M	T	W	T	F	S
					1	2
3	4	5	6	7	8	9
10	11	12	13	14	15	16
17	18	19	20	21	22	23
24	25	26	27	28	29	30

You are more than your heartache. And God has good things planned for you on the other side of the tragedy. Trust Him today. He's going to take care of you today—and always.

to-do list

- [ ] ....
- [ ] ....
- [ ] ....
- [ ] ....
- [ ] ....
- [ ] ....
- [ ] ....
- [ ] ....
- [ ] ....
- [ ] ....
- [ ] ....
- [ ] ....
- [ ] ....
- [ ] ....
- [ ] ....
- [ ] ....
- [ ] ....
- [ ] ....

SUNDAY, September 3

....
....
....
....
....

MONDAY, September 4   *Labor Day*

....
....
....
....
....

TUESDAY, September 5

....
....
....
....
....

WEDNESDAY, September 6

....
....
....
....
....

THURSDAY, September 7

....
....
....
....

FRIDAY, September 8

....
....
....
....

SATURDAY, September 9

....
....
....
....
....

to-do list

☐ ....
☐ ....
☐ ....
☐ ....
☐ ....
☐ ....
☐ ....
☐ ....
☐ ....
☐ ....
☐ ....
☐ ....
☐ ....
☐ ....
☐ ....
☐ ....
☐ ....
☐ ....

*The LORD is close to
the brokenhearted; he
rescues those whose
spirits are crushed.*
PSALM 34:18 NLT

September 2023

S	M	T	W	T	F	S
					1	2
3	4	5	6	7	8	9
10	11	12	13	14	15	16
17	18	19	20	21	22	23
24	25	26	27	28	29	30

Powerful prayers should be part of your DNA. God created you to communicate with Him. So don't just scratch the surface; commit to a genuine encounter with Him every time you pray.

to-do list

- [ ] ....
- [ ] ....
- [ ] ....
- [ ] ....
- [ ] ....
- [ ] ....
- [ ] ....
- [ ] ....
- [ ] ....
- [ ] ....
- [ ] ....
- [ ] ....
- [ ] ....
- [ ] ....
- [ ] ....
- [ ] ....
- [ ] ....

SUNDAY, September 10

MONDAY, September 11

TUESDAY, September 12

WEDNESDAY, September 13

....
....
....
....
....

THURSDAY, September 14

....
....
....
....
....

FRIDAY, September 15

....
....
....
....
....

SATURDAY, September 16

....
....
....
....
....

to-do list

☐ ....
☐ ....
☐ ....
☐ ....
☐ ....
☐ ....
☐ ....
☐ ....
☐ ....
☐ ....
☐ ....
☐ ....
☐ ....
☐ ....
☐ ....

Therefore confess your sins to each other and pray for each other so that you may be healed. The prayer of a righteous person is powerful and effective.
JAMES 5:16 NIV

September 2023

S	M	T	W	T	F	S
					1	2
3	4	5	6	7	8	9
10	11	12	13	14	15	16
17	18	19	20	21	22	23
24	25	26	27	28	29	30

God created you to receive help in times of trouble. Even when no one around you seems to notice what's going on, He does. He sees, He cares, and He's ready to intervene.

to-do list

- [ ] ....
- [ ] ....
- [ ] ....
- [ ] ....
- [ ] ....
- [ ] ....
- [ ] ....
- [ ] ....
- [ ] ....
- [ ] ....
- [ ] ....
- [ ] ....
- [ ] ....
- [ ] ....
- [ ] ....
- [ ] ....
- [ ] ....
- [ ] ....

SUNDAY, September 17

....
....
....
....
....

MONDAY, September 18

....
....
....
....
....

TUESDAY, September 19

....
....
....
....
....

WEDNESDAY, September 20

....

....

....

....

....

THURSDAY, September 21

....

....

....

....

....

FRIDAY, September 22

....

....

....

....

....

SATURDAY, September 23   *First Day of Autumn*

....

....

....

....

....

to-do list

☐ ....
☐ ....
☐ ....
☐ ....
☐ ....
☐ ....
☐ ....
☐ ....
☐ ....
☐ ....
☐ ....
☐ ....
☐ ....
☐ ....
☐ ....
☐ ....
☐ ....

*God is our refuge
and strength, an ever-
present help in trouble.*
PSALM 46:1 NIV

September 2023

S	M	T	W	T	F	S
					1	2
3	4	5	6	7	8	9
10	11	12	13	14	15	16
17	18	19	20	21	22	23
24	25	26	27	28	29	30

When we gain an eternal perspective—when we see all of life through the lens of eternity—how our perspective shifts! Suddenly, the troubles of this life are minuscule in comparison to the joy that is to come.

to-do list

- [ ]
- [ ]
- [ ]
- [ ]
- [ ]
- [ ]
- [ ]
- [ ]
- [ ]
- [ ]
- [ ]
- [ ]
- [ ]
- [ ]
- [ ]
- [ ]
- [ ]
- [ ]

SUNDAY, September 24

MONDAY, September 25

TUESDAY, September 26

WEDNESDAY, September 27

....
....
....
....
....

THURSDAY, September 28

....
....
....
....
....

FRIDAY, September 29

....
....
....
....
....

SATURDAY, September 30

....
....
....
....
....

☐ ....
☐ ....
☐ ....
☐ ....
☐ ....
☐ ....
☐ ....
☐ ....
☐ ....
☐ ....
☐ ....
☐ ....
☐ ....
☐ ....
☐ ....
☐ ....
☐ ....
☐ ....

*For I consider that
the sufferings of this
present time are not
worth comparing with
the glory that is to
be revealed to us.*
ROMANS 8:18 ESV

October 2023

SUNDAY	MONDAY	TUESDAY	WEDNESDAY
1	2	3	4
8	9 *Columbus Day*	10	11
15	16	17	18
22	23	24	25
29	30	31 *Halloween*	1

THURSDAY	FRIDAY	SATURDAY
5	6	7
12	13	14
19	20	21
26	27	28
2	3	4

notes

....
....
....
....
....
....
....
....
....
....
....
....
....
....

SEPTEMBER

S	M	T	W	T	F	S
					1	2
3	4	5	6	7	8	9
10	11	12	13	14	15	16
17	18	19	20	21	22	23
24	25	26	27	28	29	30

NOVEMBER

S	M	T	W	T	F	S
			1	2	3	4
5	6	7	8	9	10	11
12	13	14	15	16	17	18
19	20	21	22	23	24	25
26	27	28	29	30		

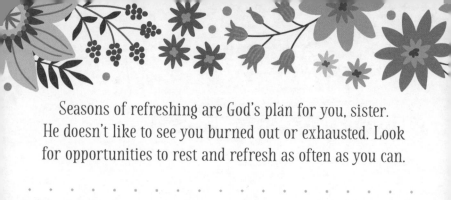

Seasons of refreshing are God's plan for you, sister. He doesn't like to see you burned out or exhausted. Look for opportunities to rest and refresh as often as you can.

Goals *for* This Month

*He refreshes my soul. He guides me along
the right paths for his name's sake.*

PSALM 23:3 NIV

October 2023

S	M	T	W	T	F	S
1	2	3	4	5	6	7
8	9	10	11	12	13	14
15	16	17	18	19	20	21
22	23	24	25	26	27	28
29	30	31				

The kind of work God calls you to is more fun and adventurous than anything you could have dreamed for yourself. Do it for Him—the Love of your life.

to-do list

- [ ]
- [ ]
- [ ]
- [ ]
- [ ]
- [ ]
- [ ]
- [ ]
- [ ]
- [ ]
- [ ]
- [ ]
- [ ]
- [ ]
- [ ]
- [ ]
- [ ]
- [ ]
- [ ]

SUNDAY, October 1

MONDAY, October 2

TUESDAY, October 3

WEDNESDAY, October 4

....
....
....
....
....

THURSDAY, October 5

....
....
....
....
....

FRIDAY, October 6

....
....
....
....
....

SATURDAY, October 7

....
....
....
....
....

to-do list

☐ ....
☐ ....
☐ ....
☐ ....
☐ ....
☐ ....
☐ ....
☐ ....
☐ ....
☐ ....
☐ ....
☐ ....
☐ ....
☐ ....
☐ ....

I have been crucified with Christ and I no longer live, but Christ lives in me. The life I now live in the body, I live by faith in the Son of God, who loved me and gave himself for me.
GALATIANS 2:20 NIV

October 2023

S	M	T	W	T	F	S
1	2	3	4	5	6	7
8	9	10	11	12	13	14
15	16	17	18	19	20	21
22	23	24	25	26	27	28
29	30	31				

God designed you to be an overcomer. He doesn't want you to give up without a fight. So keep going, girl! Lift your head high, and keep on marching even when the enemy threatens.

to-do list

- ☐ ....
- ☐ ....
- ☐ ....
- ☐ ....
- ☐ ....
- ☐ ....
- ☐ ....
- ☐ ....
- ☐ ....
- ☐ ....
- ☐ ....
- ☐ ....
- ☐ ....
- ☐ ....
- ☐ ....
- ☐ ....
- ☐ ....
- ☐ ....

SUNDAY, October 8

....
....
....
....
....

MONDAY, October 9   *Columbus Day*

....
....
....
....
....

TUESDAY, October 10

....
....
....
....
....

WEDNESDAY, October 11

- [ ] ....
- [ ] ....
- [ ] ....
- [ ] ....
- [ ] ....
- [ ] ....

THURSDAY, October 12

- [ ] ....
- [ ] ....
- [ ] ....
- [ ] ....
- [ ] ....
- [ ] ....

FRIDAY, October 13

- [ ] ....
- [ ] ....
- [ ] ....

SATURDAY, October 14

"I have told you these things, so that in me you may have peace. In this world you will have trouble. But take heart! I have overcome the world."
JOHN 16:33 NIV

October 2023

S	M	T	W	T	F	S
1	2	3	4	5	6	7
8	9	10	11	12	13	14
15	16	17	18	19	20	21
22	23	24	25	26	27	28
29	30	31				

God created you to live in peace
and harmony, and the only way
for that to happen is by following
His plan for order in your life.

to-do list

- ☐ ....
- ☐ ....
- ☐ ....
- ☐ ....
- ☐ ....
- ☐ ....
- ☐ ....
- ☐ ....
- ☐ ....
- ☐ ....
- ☐ ....
- ☐ ....
- ☐ ....
- ☐ ....
- ☐ ....
- ☐ ....
- ☐ ....
- ☐ ....
- ☐ ....

SUNDAY, October 15

....
....
....
....
....

MONDAY, October 16

....
....
....
....
....

TUESDAY, October 17

....
....
....
....
....

WEDNESDAY, October 18

....
....
....
....
....

THURSDAY, October 19

....
....
....
....
....

FRIDAY, October 20

....
....
....
....
....

SATURDAY, October 21

....
....
....
....
....

to-do list

☐ ....
☐ ....
☐ ....
☐ ....
☐ ....
☐ ....
☐ ....
☐ ....
☐ ....
☐ ....
☐ ....
☐ ....
☐ ....
☐ ....
☐ ....

*Blessed is the man
who walks not in the
counsel of the wicked,
nor stands in the way
of sinners, nor sits in
the seat of scoffers; but
his delight is in the law
of the LORD, and on
his law he meditates
day and night.*
PSALM 1:1-2 ESV

October 2023

S	M	T	W	T	F	S
1	2	3	4	5	6	7
8	9	10	11	12	13	14
15	16	17	18	19	20	21
22	23	24	25	26	27	28
29	30	31				

Be the light. *Shine* the light.
Don't be afraid to speak up,
especially in hard times.

to-do list

- [ ]
- [ ]
- [ ]
- [ ]
- [ ]
- [ ]
- [ ]
- [ ]
- [ ]
- [ ]
- [ ]
- [ ]
- [ ]
- [ ]
- [ ]
- [ ]
- [ ]
- [ ]

SUNDAY, October 22

MONDAY, October 23

TUESDAY, October 24

WEDNESDAY, October 25

to-do list

- [ ] ....
- [ ] ....

THURSDAY, October 26

- [ ] ....
- [ ] ....
- [ ] ....
- [ ] ....
- [ ] ....
- [ ] ....
- [ ] ....
- [ ] ....
- [ ] ....

FRIDAY, October 27

- [ ] ....
- [ ] ....
- [ ] ....
- [ ] ....
- [ ] ....
- [ ] ....

SATURDAY, October 28

"Then the righteous will shine like the sun in the kingdom of their Father. Whoever has ears, let them hear."
MATTHEW 13:43 NIV

November 2023

SUNDAY	MONDAY	TUESDAY	WEDNESDAY
29	30	31	1
5 *Daylight Saving Time Ends*	6	7 *Election Day*	8
12	13	14	15
19	20	21	22
26	27	28	29

notes

THURSDAY	FRIDAY	SATURDAY
2	3	4
9	10	11 *Veterans Day*
16	17	18
23 *Thanksgiving Day*	24	25
30	1	2

....
....
....
....
....
....
....
....
....
....
....
....
....
....

OCTOBER

S	M	T	W	T	F	S
1	2	3	4	5	6	7
8	9	10	11	12	13	14
15	16	17	18	19	20	21
22	23	24	25	26	27	28
29	30	31				

DECEMBER

S	M	T	W	T	F	S
					1	2
3	4	5	6	7	8	9
10	11	12	13	14	15	16
17	18	19	20	21	22	23
24	25	26	27	28	29	30
31						

God adores you. He's the perfect Master, one you can trust—totally, fully, and completely!

Goals *for* This Month

Let us then with confidence draw near to the throne of grace,
that we may receive mercy and find grace to help in time of need.
HEBREWS 4:16 ESV

October–November 2023

S	M	T	W	T	F	S
			1	2	3	4
5	6	7	8	9	10	11
12	13	14	15	16	17	18
19	20	21	22	23	24	25
26	27	28	29	30		

Be faithful in your giving, and God will bless you in ways you never saw coming.

to-do list

- [ ] ....
- [ ] ....
- [ ] ....
- [ ] ....
- [ ] ....
- [ ] ....
- [ ] ....
- [ ] ....
- [ ] ....
- [ ] ....
- [ ] ....
- [ ] ....
- [ ] ....
- [ ] ....
- [ ] ....
- [ ] ....
- [ ] ....
- [ ] ....

SUNDAY, October 29

MONDAY, October 30

TUESDAY, October 31   *Halloween*

WEDNESDAY, November 1

....
....
....
....
....

THURSDAY, November 2

....
....
....
....
....

FRIDAY, November 3

....
....
....
....

SATURDAY, November 4

....
....
....
....
....

to-do list

☐ ....
☐ ....
☐ ....
☐ ....
☐ ....
☐ ....
☐ ....
☐ ....
☐ ....
☐ ....
☐ ....
☐ ....
☐ ....

"Bring the full tithe into the storehouse, that there may be food in my house. And thereby put me to the test, says the LORD of hosts, if I will not open the windows of heaven for you and pour down for you a blessing until there is no more need."

MALACHI 3:10 ESV

November 2023

S	M	T	W	T	F	S
			1	2	3	4
5	6	7	8	9	10	11
12	13	14	15	16	17	18
19	20	21	22	23	24	25
26	27	28	29	30		

What are you thirsting for today? What has caused you to become parched and dry? Head to the river, and wait in hopeful expectation as God replenishes your soul and gives you all you need for the journey.

to-do list

- [ ] ....
- [ ] ....
- [ ] ....
- [ ] ....
- [ ] ....
- [ ] ....
- [ ] ....
- [ ] ....
- [ ] ....
- [ ] ....
- [ ] ....
- [ ] ....
- [ ] ....
- [ ] ....
- [ ] ....
- [ ] ....
- [ ] ....
- [ ] ....

SUNDAY, November 5 *Daylight Saving Time Ends*

....
....
....
....
....

MONDAY, November 6

....
....
....
....
....

TUESDAY, November 7 *Election Day*

....
....
....
....
....

WEDNESDAY, November 8

....
....
....
....
....

THURSDAY, November 9

....
....
....
....
....

FRIDAY, November 10

....
....
....
....
....

SATURDAY, November 11   *Veterans Day*

....
....
....
....
....

to-do list

- [ ] ....
- [ ] ....
- [ ] ....
- [ ] ....
- [ ] ....
- [ ] ....
- [ ] ....
- [ ] ....
- [ ] ....
- [ ] ....
- [ ] ....
- [ ] ....
- [ ] ....
- [ ] ....

"Remember not the former things, nor consider the things of old. Behold, I am doing a new thing; now it springs forth, do you not perceive it? I will make a way in the wilderness and rivers in the desert."

ISAIAH 43:18-19 ESV

November 2023

S	M	T	W	T	F	S
			1	2	3	4
5	6	7	8	9	10	11
12	13	14	15	16	17	18
19	20	21	22	23	24	25
26	27	28	29	30		

You were made for deep roots, girl—deeper and deeper still as you grow in your faith. Don't let the storms of life topple you. You were meant to stand strong.

to-do list

- [ ]
- [ ]
- [ ]
- [ ]
- [ ]
- [ ]
- [ ]
- [ ]
- [ ]
- [ ]
- [ ]
- [ ]
- [ ]
- [ ]
- [ ]
- [ ]
- [ ]
- [ ]

SUNDAY, November 12

MONDAY, November 13

TUESDAY, November 14

WEDNESDAY, November 15

....
....
....
....
....

THURSDAY, November 16

....
....
....
....
....

FRIDAY, November 17

....
....
....
....
....

SATURDAY, November 18

....
....
....
....
....

to-do list

- [ ] ....
- [ ] ....
- [ ] ....
- [ ] ....
- [ ] ....
- [ ] ....
- [ ] ....
- [ ] ....
- [ ] ....
- [ ] ....
- [ ] ....
- [ ] ....
- [ ] ....
- [ ] ....

I pray that out of his glorious riches he may strengthen you with power through his Spirit in your inner being, so that Christ may dwell in your hearts through faith. And I pray that you [may be] rooted and established in love.

EPHESIANS 3:16-17 NIV

November 2023

S	M	T	W	T	F	S
			1	2	3	4
5	6	7	8	9	10	11
12	13	14	15	16	17	18
19	20	21	22	23	24	25
26	27	28	29	30		

Deep breath, girl. Gather your thoughts. Make your requests known to God. He's right there waiting to meet you at your point of need.

to-do list

- ☐ ....
- ☐ ....
- ☐ ....
- ☐ ....
- ☐ ....
- ☐ ....
- ☐ ....
- ☐ ....
- ☐ ....
- ☐ ....
- ☐ ....
- ☐ ....
- ☐ ....
- ☐ ....
- ☐ ....
- ☐ ....
- ☐ ....
- ☐ ....

SUNDAY, November 19

....
....
....
....
....

MONDAY, November 20

....
....
....
....
....

TUESDAY, November 21

....
....
....
....
....

WEDNESDAY, November 22

☐ ....

☐ ....

☐ ....

☐ ....

THURSDAY, November 23   *Thanksgiving Day*

☐ ....

☐ ....

☐ ....

☐ ....

☐ ....

☐ ....

FRIDAY, November 24

☐ ....

☐ ....

☐ ....

SATURDAY, November 25

Do not be anxious about anything, but in everything by prayer and supplication with thanksgiving let your requests be made known to God.

PHILIPPIANS 4:6 ESV

November–December 2023

S	M	T	W	T	F	S
			1	2	3	4
5	6	7	8	9	10	11
12	13	14	15	16	17	18
19	20	21	22	23	24	25
26	27	28	29	30		

Trust the heavenly Father in the scary seasons. Keep your eyes wide open. More help is coming your way as long as you look to Him and trust His guidance.

to-do list

☐ ....
☐ ....
☐ ....
☐ ....
☐ ....
☐ ....
☐ ....
☐ ....
☐ ....
☐ ....
☐ ....
☐ ....
☐ ....
☐ ....
☐ ....
☐ ....
☐ ....
☐ ....

SUNDAY, November 26

....
....
....
....
....

MONDAY, November 27

....
....
....
....
....

TUESDAY, November 28

....
....
....
....
....

WEDNESDAY, November 29

....

....

....

....

....

THURSDAY, November 30

....

....

....

....

....

FRIDAY, December 1

....

....

....

....

....

SATURDAY, December 2

....

....

....

....

....

to-do list

- [ ] ....
- [ ] ....
- [ ] ....
- [ ] ....
- [ ] ....
- [ ] ....
- [ ] ....
- [ ] ....
- [ ] ....
- [ ] ....
- [ ] ....
- [ ] ....
- [ ] ....
- [ ] ....
- [ ] ....

Fear not, for I am with you; be not dismayed, for I am your God; I will strengthen you, I will help you, I will uphold you with my righteous right hand."
ISAIAH 41:10 ESV

December 2023

SUNDAY	MONDAY	TUESDAY	WEDNESDAY
26	27	28	29
3	4	5	6
10	11	12	13
17	18	19	20
24 *Christmas Eve* / *New Year's Eve* 31	25 *Christmas Day*	26	27

notes

THURSDAY	FRIDAY	SATURDAY
30	1	2
7	8	9
Hanukkah Begins at Sundown		
14	15	16
21	22	23
First Day of Winter		
28	29	30

....
....
....
....
....
....
....
....
....
....
....
....
....
....

NOVEMBER

S	M	T	W	T	F	S
			1	2	3	4
5	6	7	8	9	10	11
12	13	14	15	16	17	18
19	20	21	22	23	24	25
26	27	28	29	30		

JANUARY

S	M	T	W	T	F	S
	1	2	3	4	5	6
7	8	9	10	11	12	13
14	15	16	17	18	19	20
21	22	23	24	25	26	27
28	29	30	31			

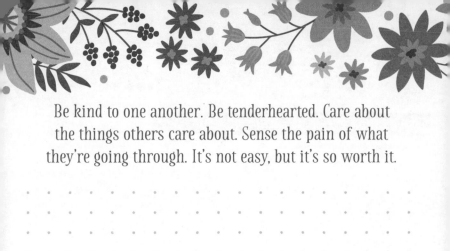

Be kind to one another. Be tenderhearted. Care about the things others care about. Sense the pain of what they're going through. It's not easy, but it's so worth it.

Goals *for* This Month

. . . .
. . . .
. . . .
. . . .
. . . .
. . . .
. . . .
. . . .
. . . .
. . . .
. . . .
. . . .
. . . .
. . . .
. . . .
. . . .
. . . .
. . . .
. . . .
. . . .
. . . .
. . . .
. . . .

Be kind to one another, tenderhearted, forgiving
one another, as God in Christ forgave you.

EPHESIANS 4:32 ESV

December 2023

S	M	T	W	T	F	S
					1	2
3	4	5	6	7	8	9
10	11	12	13	14	15	16
17	18	19	20	21	22	23
24	25	26	27	28	29	30
31						

What's pulling you under today?
What has you the most weighed
down? Trust God to deliver you and
set your feet on solid ground.

to-do list

- [ ] ....
- [ ] ....
- [ ] ....
- [ ] ....
- [ ] ....
- [ ] ....
- [ ] ....
- [ ] ....
- [ ] ....
- [ ] ....
- [ ] ....
- [ ] ....
- [ ] ....
- [ ] ....
- [ ] ....
- [ ] ....
- [ ] ....
- [ ] ....
- [ ] ....
- [ ] ....

SUNDAY, December 3

MONDAY, December 4

TUESDAY, December 5

WEDNESDAY, December 6

....
....
....
....
....

THURSDAY, December 7 *Hanukkah Begins at Sundown*

....
....
....
....
....

FRIDAY, December 8

....
....
....
....
....

SATURDAY, December 9

....
....
....
....
....

to-do list

- [ ] ....
- [ ] ....
- [ ] ....
- [ ] ....
- [ ] ....
- [ ] ....
- [ ] ....
- [ ] ....
- [ ] ....
- [ ] ....
- [ ] ....
- [ ] ....
- [ ] ....
- [ ] ....
- [ ] ....
- [ ] ....
- [ ] ....

*When the righteous cry
for help, the LORD hears
and delivers them out
of all their troubles.*
PSALM 34:17 ESV

December 2023

S	M	T	W	T	F	S
					1	2
3	4	5	6	7	8	9
10	11	12	13	14	15	16
17	18	19	20	21	22	23
24	25	26	27	28	29	30
31						

When you grab hold of the Lord's peace, you let go of anything else that's threatening to hold you back. In many ways, it's like taking hold of a life raft. You have to cling to it for dear life and never let it go.

to-do list

- [ ] ....
- [ ] ....
- [ ] ....
- [ ] ....
- [ ] ....
- [ ] ....
- [ ] ....
- [ ] ....
- [ ] ....
- [ ] ....
- [ ] ....
- [ ] ....
- [ ] ....
- [ ] ....
- [ ] ....
- [ ] ....
- [ ] ....
- [ ] ....

SUNDAY, December 10

MONDAY, December 11

TUESDAY, December 12

WEDNESDAY, December 13

....
....
....
....
....

THURSDAY, December 14

....
....
....
....
....

FRIDAY, December 15

....
....
....
....
....

SATURDAY, December 16

....
....
....
....
....

to-do list

- [ ] ....
- [ ] ....
- [ ] ....
- [ ] ....
- [ ] ....
- [ ] ....
- [ ] ....
- [ ] ....
- [ ] ....
- [ ] ....
- [ ] ....
- [ ] ....
- [ ] ....
- [ ] ....
- [ ] ....
- [ ] ....
- [ ] ....
- [ ] ....

*Let him turn away
from evil and do
good; let him seek
peace and pursue it.*
1 PETER 3:11 ESV

December 2023

S	M	T	W	T	F	S
					1	2
3	4	5	6	7	8	9
10	11	12	13	14	15	16
17	18	19	20	21	22	23
24	25	26	27	28	29	30
31						

The Lord has promised to be your stronghold in times of trouble. When everything else is crumbling, He won't.

to-do list

- [ ]
- [ ]
- [ ]
- [ ]
- [ ]
- [ ]
- [ ]
- [ ]
- [ ]
- [ ]
- [ ]
- [ ]
- [ ]
- [ ]
- [ ]
- [ ]
- [ ]
- [ ]

SUNDAY, December 17

MONDAY, December 18

TUESDAY, December 19

WEDNESDAY, December 20

....
....
....
....
....

THURSDAY, December 21   *First Day of Winter*

....
....
....
....
....

FRIDAY, December 22

....
....
....
....
....

SATURDAY, December 23

....
....
....
....
....

to-do list

- [ ] ....
- [ ] ....
- [ ] ....
- [ ] ....
- [ ] ....
- [ ] ....
- [ ] ....
- [ ] ....
- [ ] ....
- [ ] ....
- [ ] ....
- [ ] ....
- [ ] ....
- [ ] ....
- [ ] ....
- [ ] ....
- [ ] ....

*The LORD is a
stronghold for the
oppressed, a stronghold
in times of trouble.*
PSALM 9:9 ESV

December 2023

S	M	T	W	T	F	S
					1	2
3	4	5	6	7	8	9
10	11	12	13	14	15	16
17	18	19	20	21	22	23
24	25	26	27	28	29	30
31						

God designed you to operate in a family. It's where you can thrive, be encouraged, and even fail with grace sometimes.

to-do list

- [ ] ....
- [ ] ....
- [ ] ....
- [ ] ....
- [ ] ....
- [ ] ....
- [ ] ....
- [ ] ....
- [ ] ....
- [ ] ....
- [ ] ....
- [ ] ....
- [ ] ....
- [ ] ....
- [ ] ....
- [ ] ....
- [ ] ....
- [ ] ....

SUNDAY, December 24   *Christmas Eve*

MONDAY, December 25   *Christmas Day*

TUESDAY, December 26

WEDNESDAY, December 27

....
....
....
....
....

THURSDAY, December 28

....
....
....
....
....

FRIDAY, December 29

....
....
....
....
....

SATURDAY, December 30

....
....
....
....
....

to-do list

☐ ....
☐ ....
☐ ....
☐ ....
☐ ....
☐ ....
☐ ....
☐ ....
☐ ....
☐ ....
☐ ....
☐ ....
☐ ....
☐ ....
☐ ....
☐ ....
☐ ....
☐ ....

God sets the lonely in families, he leads out the prisoners with singing; but the rebellious live in a sun-scorched land.
PSALM 68:6 NIV

December 2023–January 2024

S	M	T	W	T	F	S
					1	2
3	4	5	6	7	8	9
10	11	12	13	14	15	16
17	18	19	20	21	22	23
24	25	26	27	28	29	30
31						

You were made for more courage, girl. More and more and more. So square those shoulders. Don't let those wobbly knees worry you. God's got this. And with your hand in His, you've got it too.

to-do list

- [ ]
- [ ]
- [ ]
- [ ]
- [ ]
- [ ]
- [ ]
- [ ]
- [ ]
- [ ]
- [ ]
- [ ]
- [ ]
- [ ]
- [ ]
- [ ]
- [ ]
- [ ]

SUNDAY, December 31 *New Year's Eve*

MONDAY, January 1 *New Year's Day*

TUESDAY, January 2

WEDNESDAY, January 3

....

....

....

....

....

THURSDAY, January 4

....

....

....

....

....

FRIDAY, January 5

....

....

....

....

....

SATURDAY, January 6

....

....

....

....

....

to-do list

☐ ....
☐ ....
☐ ....
☐ ....
☐ ....
☐ ....
☐ ....
☐ ....
☐ ....
☐ ....
☐ ....
☐ ....
☐ ....
☐ ....
☐ ....
☐ ....
☐ ....

*"Have I not commanded
you? Be strong and
courageous. Do not
be afraid; do not
be discouraged, for
the LORD your God
will be with you
wherever you go."*
JOSHUA 1:9 NIV

CONTACTS

Name:

Address:

Phone: Mobile:

E-mail:

Name:

Address:

Phone: Mobile:

E-mail:

Name:

Address:

Phone: Mobile:

E-mail:

Name:

Address:

Phone: Mobile:

E-mail:

CONTACTS

Name:

Address:

Phone: Mobile:

E-mail:

Name:

Address:

Phone: Mobilé:

E-mail:

Name:

Address:

Phone: Mobile:

E-mail:

Name:

Address:

Phone: Mobile:

E-mail:

CONTACTS

Name:

Address:

Phone: Mobile:

E-mail:

Name:

Address:

Phone: Mobile:

E-mail:

Name:

Address:

Phone: Mobile:

E-mail:

Name:

Address:

Phone: Mobile:

E-mail:

CONTACTS

Name:

Address:

Phone: Mobile:

E-mail:

Name:

Address:

Phone: Mobile:

E-mail:

Name:

Address:

Phone: Mobile:

E-mail:

Name:

Address:

Phone: Mobile:

E-mail:

CONTACTS

Name:

Address:

Phone: Mobile:

E-mail:

Name:

Address:

Phone: Mobile:

E-mail:

Name:

Address:

Phone: Mobile:

E-mail:

Name:

Address:

Phone: Mobile:

E-mail:

CONTACTS

Name:

Address:

Phone: Mobile:

E-mail:

Name:

Address:

Phone: Mobile:

E-mail:

Name:

Address:

Phone: Mobile:

E-mail:

Name:

Address:

Phone: Mobile:

E-mail:

CONTACTS

Name:

Address:

Phone: Mobile:

E-mail:

Name:

Address:

Phone: Mobile:

E-mail:

Name:

Address:

Phone: Mobile:

E-mail:

Name:

Address:

Phone: Mobile:

E-mail:

CONTACTS

Name:

Address:

Phone: Mobile:

E-mail:

Name:

Address:

Phone: Mobile:

E-mail:

Name:

Address:

Phone: Mobile:

E-mail:

Name:

Address:

Phone: Mobile:

E-mail:

CONTACTS

Name:

Address:

Phone: Mobile:

E-mail:

Name:

Address:

Phone: Mobile:

E-mail:

Name:

Address:

Phone: Mobile:

E-mail:

Name:

Address:

Phone: Mobile:

E-mail:

CONTACTS

Name:

Address:

Phone: Mobile:

E-mail:

Name:

Address:

Phone: Mobile:

E-mail:

Name:

Address:

Phone: Mobile:

E-mail:

Name:

Address:

Phone: Mobile:

E-mail:

CONTACTS

Name:

Address:

Phone: Mobile:

E-mail:

Name:

Address:

Phone: Mobile:

E-mail:

Name:

Address:

Phone: Mobile:

E-mail:

Name:

Address:

Phone: Mobile:

E-mail:

CONTACTS

Name:

Address:

Phone: Mobile:

E-mail:

Name:

Address:

Phone: Mobile:

E-mail:

Name:

Address:

Phone: Mobile:

E-mail:

Name:

Address:

Phone: Mobile:

E-mail:

CONTACTS

Name:

Address:

Phone: Mobile:

E-mail:

Name:

Address:

Phone: Mobile:

E-mail:

Name:

Address:

Phone: Mobile:

E-mail:

Name:

Address:

Phone: Mobile:

E-mail:

CONTACTS

Name:

Address:

Phone: Mobile:

E-mail:

Name:

Address:

Phone: Mobile:

E-mail:

Name:

Address:

Phone: Mobile:

E-mail:

Name:

Address:

Phone: Mobile:

E-mail:

2024

JANUARY
S	M	T	W	T	F	S
	1	2	3	4	5	6
7	8	9	10	11	12	13
14	15	16	17	18	19	20
21	22	23	24	25	26	27
28	29	30	31			

FEBRUARY
S	M	T	W	T	F	S
				1	2	3
4	5	6	7	8	9	10
11	12	13	14	15	16	17
18	19	20	21	22	23	24
25	26	27	28	29		

MARCH
S	M	T	W	T	F	S
					1	2
3	4	5	6	7	8	9
10	11	12	13	14	15	16
17	18	19	20	21	22	23
24	25	26	27	28	29	30
31						

APRIL
S	M	T	W	T	F	S
	1	2	3	4	5	6
7	8	9	10	11	12	13
14	15	16	17	18	19	20
21	22	23	24	25	26	27
28	29	30				

MAY
S	M	T	W	T	F	S
			1	2	3	4
5	6	7	8	9	10	11
12	13	14	15	16	17	18
19	20	21	22	23	24	25
26	27	28	29	30	31	

JUNE
S	M	T	W	T	F	S
						1
2	3	4	5	6	7	8
9	10	11	12	13	14	15
16	17	18	19	20	21	22
23	24	25	26	27	28	29
30						

JULY
S	M	T	W	T	F	S
	1	2	3	4	5	6
7	8	9	10	11	12	13
14	15	16	17	18	19	20
21	22	23	24	25	26	27
28	29	30	31			

AUGUST
S	M	T	W	T	F	S
				1	2	3
4	5	6	7	8	9	10
11	12	13	14	15	16	17
18	19	20	21	22	23	24
25	26	27	28	29	30	31

SEPTEMBER
S	M	T	W	T	F	S
1	2	3	4	5	6	7
8	9	10	11	12	13	14
15	16	17	18	19	20	21
22	23	24	25	26	27	28
29	30					

OCTOBER
S	M	T	W	T	F	S
		1	2	3	4	5
6	7	8	9	10	11	12
13	14	15	16	17	18	19
20	21	22	23	24	25	26
27	28	29	30	31		

NOVEMBER
S	M	T	W	T	F	S
					1	2
3	4	5	6	7	8	9
10	11	12	13	14	15	16
17	18	19	20	21	22	23
24	25	26	27	28	29	30

DECEMBER
S	M	T	W	T	F	S
1	2	3	4	5	6	7
8	9	10	11	12	13	14
15	16	17	18	19	20	21
22	23	24	25	26	27	28
29	30	31				

2025

JANUARY
S	M	T	W	T	F	S
			1	2	3	4
5	6	7	8	9	10	11
12	13	14	15	16	17	18
19	20	21	22	23	24	25
26	27	28	29	30	31	

FEBRUARY
S	M	T	W	T	F	S
						1
2	3	4	5	6	7	8
9	10	11	12	13	14	15
16	17	18	19	20	21	22
23	24	25	26	27	28	

MARCH
S	M	T	W	T	F	S
						1
2	3	4	5	6	7	8
9	10	11	12	13	14	15
16	17	18	19	20	21	22
23	24	25	26	27	28	29
30	31					

APRIL
S	M	T	W	T	F	S
		1	2	3	4	5
6	7	8	9	10	11	12
13	14	15	16	17	18	19
20	21	22	23	24	25	26
27	28	29	30			

MAY
S	M	T	W	T	F	S
				1	2	3
4	5	6	7	8	9	10
11	12	13	14	15	16	17
18	19	20	21	22	23	24
25	26	27	28	29	30	31

JUNE
S	M	T	W	T	F	S
1	2	3	4	5	6	7
8	9	10	11	12	13	14
15	16	17	18	19	20	21
22	23	24	25	26	27	28
29	30					

JULY
S	M	T	W	T	F	S
		1	2	3	4	5
6	7	8	9	10	11	12
13	14	15	16	17	18	19
20	21	22	23	24	25	26
27	28	29	30	31		

AUGUST
S	M	T	W	T	F	S
					1	2
3	4	5	6	7	8	9
10	11	12	13	14	15	16
17	18	19	20	21	22	23
24	25	26	27	28	29	30
31						

SEPTEMBER
S	M	T	W	T	F	S
	1	2	3	4	5	6
7	8	9	10	11	12	13
14	15	16	17	18	19	20
21	22	23	24	25	26	27
28	29	30				

OCTOBER
S	M	T	W	T	F	S
			1	2	3	4
5	6	7	8	9	10	11
12	13	14	15	16	17	18
19	20	21	22	23	24	25
26	27	28	29	30	31	

NOVEMBER
S	M	T	W	T	F	S
						1
2	3	4	5	6	7	8
9	10	11	12	13	14	15
16	17	18	19	20	21	22
23	24	25	26	27	28	29
30						

DECEMBER
S	M	T	W	T	F	S
	1	2	3	4	5	6
7	8	9	10	11	12	13
14	15	16	17	18	19	20
21	22	23	24	25	26	27
28	29	30	31			